In Honor of

Judy Cawthorne

Presented by

Jeanne Blaes

KariAnne's oh-so-relatable stories and hysterical tales of her everyday mishaps and grand adventures had me doubled over in laughter (while trying to keep the mascara from smearing down my face). The heart lessons found in the journey will inspire everyone who (like me!) finds themselves in this "so close to amazing" sisterhood.

MELISSA MICHAELS
New York Times bestselling author of *Love the Home You Have* and *The Inspired Room* blog

Friendship is something that happens when two people say, "Me, too," and KariAnne has a way of reminding you that you're not the only one. Her honest, real, relatable approach to life is refreshing for her audience in so many ways. *So Close to Amazing* had me in fits of laughter, paired with unexpected tears that come only when someone is so honest with their own struggles and unexpected twists in life. It's here that she reminds us in her own one-of-a-kind way not to miss the little moments. Because it's in the little moments that the most beautiful ones are unexpectedly found.

ASHLEY MILLS
thehandmadehome.net

So Close to Amazing is a reminder that life is never perfect, always changing, and ever evolving, and that with faith, we can overcome the obstacles that simply living life brings our way. KariAnne invites readers into her witty and wonderfully wacky world of moving to the country in Kentucky with her husband and four children, with its challenges of fitting in to a new place. With the humor and humility she lives out in everyday life, she's a friend you want to sit down and have coffee with, who would be fun to do a DIY project with, and who speaks to the hearts of real women everywhere.

RHODA VICKERS
southernhospitalityblog.com

KariAnne doesn't know it yet, but she's my new BFF. She's hilarious, honest, and the perfect kind of hot mess who lets you know you're not alone. At the risk of stating the obvious, *So Close to Amazing* isn't close to amazing. It *is* amazing. You'll find yourself cheering for KariAnne through every mishap—and thanking God for loving each of us as we are. You get more than a book with *So Close to Amazing*. You get heartfelt stories, great DIY projects, and a new BFF.

JENNIFER DUKES LEE
Author of *The Happiness Dare* and *Love Idol*

I love KariAnne's story, and I wish we all lived so boldly, with a measure of her energy and passion and humor and faith. She is a treasure.

EDIE WADSWORTH
Author of *All The Pretty Things*; *lifeingraceblog.com*

One part memoir and one part afternoon on the porch with a friend (with sweet tea in hand!), *So Close to Amazing* offers us fresh perspective on our own twists and turns in life . . . and delivers those life lessons through KariAnne's signature wit and charm.

RUTH CHOU SIMONS
Author of *GraceLaced: Discovering Timeless Truths through Seasons of the Heart* and founder of *gracelaced.com*

Each page is filled with KariAnne's genuine enthusiasm, mind-blowing optimism, and humble faith. It is an entertaining reminder of the power of believing you are amazing, even when you miss the mark by a little bit, and the power of remembering to put it in his hands.

LAURA PUTNAM
findinghomefarms.com

For the twelve years I've known KariAnne, she's never done anything halfway. Anything she touches is always *amazing*! This book is no different. It is an engaging, creative blend of humorous sharing about a woman's struggles on everything from fitting in to keeping faith. It will encourage you on your worst days, affirm you on your best days, and make you smile any day at all. You will join her journey from one adventure to the next and will most likely come away inspired for your next DIY project.

BRENNA STULL
Author of *Coach Mom: 7 Strategies for Organizing Your Family into an All-Star Team*

so close to amazing

so close to amazing

Stories of a DIY Life Gone Wrong . . . and Learning
to Find the Beauty in Every Imperfection

KariAnne Wood

TYNDALE
MOMENTUM™

The nonfiction imprint of
Tyndale House Publishers, Inc.

Visit Tyndale online at www.tyndale.com.

Visit Tyndale Momentum online at www.tyndalemomentum.com.

Visit the author's website at www.thistlewoodfarms.com.

TYNDALE, *Tyndale Momentum*, and Tyndale's quill logo are registered trademarks of Tyndale House Publishers, Inc. The Tyndale Momentum logo is a trademark of Tyndale House Publishers, Inc. Tyndale Momentum is the nonfiction imprint of Tyndale House Publishers, Inc., Carol Stream, Illinois.

So Close to Amazing: Stories of a DIY Life Gone Wrong . . . and Learning to Find the Beauty in Every Imperfection

Cover design by Nicole Grimes

Interior design by Jennifer Phelps

Edited by Stephanie Rische

Published in association with the literary agency of William K. Jensen Literary Agency, 119 Bampton Court, Eugene, OR 97404.

For information about special discounts for bulk purchases, please contact Tyndale House Publishers at csresponse@tyndale.com, or call 1-800-323-9400.

ISBN 978-1-4964-2201-9

Printed in the United States of America

23	22	21	20	19	18	17
7	6	5	4	3	2	1

This book is dedicated to my father. You were the one who went first. You were the writer, the poet, the listener, the teacher, and the leader of your band of merry men. I can feel your heartbeat in every line of this book. I'm lifting my pen to you in heaven. I love you, Dad.

contents

Foreword xiii

Acknowledgments xvii

Introduction: How to Be Amazing xix

1   Leap before You Look 1

2   Knock, Knock; Who's There? 19

3   I Would Move Six Hundred Miles 33

4   Every House Needs a Happily-Ever-After 51

5   Never Underestimate a Slippery Spaghetti Ring 69

6   A Floor without End 85

7   Trash-Talking 103

8   The Roast That Went to Garden Club 119

9   The Day Goliath Met a T. Rex 135

10   My Achilles Hips 151

11   Flooded with Possibilities 167

12   If You Blink, You'll Miss the French Fries 185

Epilogue 199

About the Author 201

foreword

Being asked to write the foreword to the book of an author you've never met face-to-face is the literary equivalent of being set up on a blind date in the '80s. (You know, before Christian Mingle, or swiping right or left, or the ability to cyberstalk the date before you actually meet.)

But when I found out that KariAnne wanted me to write this foreword and that she was the queen of quaint DIY, I was immediately intrigued.

You see, I'm in the middle of my own home restoration project, and I thought by reading *So Close to Amazing* I might pick up some fun and fab ideas to use in my own home. (Again, I am the blind date equivalent of meeting up with a guy who works on Wall Street in order to get stock tips. I am the worst . . .)

Just a few months into restoring my house, I realized this was more than a little fixer-upper. It was a journey into the depths of my soul. Parenting is the first level of self-discovery. A close second?

Restoring a house. Parenting magnified all the weaknesses deep in me that were already there. Restoring a house caused me to go discover the black little heart I was able to hide from the rest of the world. Dealing with faulty wiring and possible asbestos can bring that shriveled, rotted pit of a heart out in a girl.

KariAnne is the kind of person who, if you were crazy enough to do a painted wood DIY project, would have the perfect piece of wood that she found on the road six months ago and would be able to offer expert advice. Little things, like you have to "dry it out" and "spray it off" so you don't have "nests of bugs" taking up residence in your master bedroom (true story). That is the kind of friend a DIY novice needs to have in her back pocket. Designer guru? Check!

But what I didn't know was that KariAnne and I were best friends minus one tiny detail: we just hadn't met yet. And how did I know that she'd love me? Because while she confessed that she needs a wide-calf boot, I have to find an EXTRA-wide-calf boot. In a size 11. With an arch support. Basically, a unicorn standing in a field of rainbow clover. Potential best friend? Check!

And yes, in this book there are plenty of great ideas for all of us who long to DIY but have learned firsthand that it can sometimes go so wrong. KariAnne gets it. She is a gentle guide and shares her hope, visions, and challenges honestly and with enough humor that you don't feel sorry for her. You just want to be with her on all her misadventures. That is the kind of spiritual fixer-upper guide a girl like me needs.

But more than that, KariAnne is the kind of person you need by your side so that when God says, "Jump!" you have someone holding your hand to take the leap. She will hear your fears, pray for you, offer you some sweet tea, and then give you the gentle kick in the behind you need in order to do that big God-thing he is calling you to. Spiritual sister? Check!

I have become a devoted reader of her blog, *thistlewoodfarms. com*. And what do I love? That her blog, her book, and her Facebook Messenger notes all sound exactly the same. She is the same person on the pages and off the pages.

You will want her to be your best friend. But picture me with a weathered piece of wood (minus bugs) in one hand and a drapery rod made out of dowel and doorknobs in the other, warning in a low growl, "Back off! She's mine. You can't have her."

But you can read *So Close to Amazing*. And that's the next best thing.

KATHI LIPP
Author and intrepid home-restoration warrior

acknowledgments

DENTON SR.:

You are my heart. My song singer, my hand holder, my
treasure finder, and my best friend. Wherever you lead, I'll go.

DENTON JR., ZACHARY, WESTLEIGH, AND WHITNEY:

Always remember—I love you more.

MOTHER:

Thank you for being the leader of the Annes. I count it a
privilege to be one of your chicks.

ANDREA:

Thank you for lending me an ear. Thank you for inspiring
and cheering and encouraging me every page of the way.

RUTH:

Thank you for believing in me.

STEPHANIE AND SARAH:

Thank you for every note, every edit, and every verbal
exclamation point. You had me with the first ring of the gong.

INTRODUCTION

how to be amazing

I still remember the exact minute I decided I was going to be amazing.

It was the Sunday morning I debuted my very own fashion master-piece. I tromped downstairs for breakfast, valiantly trying to tame my Flock-of-Seagulls hair. With remnants of yesterday's blue eye shadow still dotting my eyelids, I walked into the room wearing a Shaun Cassidy T-shirt, sweatpants, and a bright orange scrunchie.

I was sixteen and ready to take on the world and a few ancillary planets. Plopping into the nearest chair, I rubbed the sleep (along with bits of eye shadow) from my eyes and poured myself a bowl of the breakfast of champions: Lucky Charms. Crunch went the hearts and stars and tiny marshmallows, when suddenly, midspoonful, my eyes burst open in delight.

Today was Sunday.

Today was church.

Today was the day I planned to introduce the perfect outfit to my little corner of Texas.

At eleven o'clock the night before, I'd discovered a bolt of black fabric in the craft closet and decided to sew myself a skirt to wear to church. I know. Brilliant, right? I'm not exactly sure why I decided I needed a black skirt. I'm not exactly sure why I embarked on a sewing project at almost midnight. But once I thought up the idea, I couldn't let it go. Visions of gliding into church with a new outfit to the oohs and ahhs of the gathered congregation danced in my head. I didn't have a pattern or measurements—or even the basic concept of how a skirt was actually constructed. But that wasn't going to get in my way. Minor details. Sewing speed bumps.

I knew I had this.

I started by cutting out a piece of fabric and wrapping it around me to visualize the skirt of my dreams. I stood in front of the mirror, turning this way and that, twirling and dipping, awkwardly clutching the black cotton fabric in one hand. All at once, I stopped midtwirl.

That's it! I thought as a lightbulb went on over my head. *A tube! That's what I need. A giant tube of fabric.*

I lugged out my mother's Singer sewing machine from the back recesses of the hall closet, carefully lined up the two ends of the fabric, and sewed a straight line down the middle. I turned the fabric right side out, and then I carefully wriggled into the tube and tiptoed over to the mirror to assess the progress of my sewing experiment. We were so close, my skirt and I.

And yet so far.

That's when my next brilliant idea struck.

A hem, I told the skirt. *That's what you need. A straight hem.*

I turned back to the sewing machine and added a hem, flipped my almost-skirt right side out, and tried it on again. I sighed as I stared at my reflection. *What am I missing? What's wrong?*

It really didn't look like a skirt—at least not one you'd wear in public. *What's up with the top and all that excess material?* I wondered. *And why does the tube kind of end midair with the raw edges of the material flapping around where my waist should be?*

Enter brilliant idea number three.

A waistband.

Sounds easy, right? But here's the thing. Merely adding a waistband to a black tube doesn't automatically make it look like it was designed on purpose. Especially when you invent your own jaw-dropping, once-in-a-lifetime version that the world may or may not have ever seen before. I couldn't find elastic in our craft closet, so instead I pleated the top with safety pins, gathered rolls of fabric, and fluffed them out over the pinned edge of the tube. It all totally worked if you squinted and didn't look too closely. The pleated-safety-pinned-fluffed top mimicked a waistband and still gave me enough room to wriggle in and out of the tube.

Finally, my skirt was done. I couldn't wait until my friends saw it. I couldn't wait until Sunday school. I couldn't wait to be the talk of the eleven o'clock service.

After finishing my cereal, I went upstairs to get ready. Starting with lip liner and a fresh coat of red lipstick, I applied my makeup, teased and ratted my perm to the sky, and sprayed enough Aqua Net to send rockets into outer space. At last, I turned to my skirt with all the excitement and anticipation of Christmas morning. Slowly and carefully I wriggled into it, adjusted the waistband, and topped off the ensemble with its fashion equal.

A plaid lumberjack shirt.

I tucked the ends of the shirt into the top of the skirt, poufed it over the edge, slipped on a pair of black heels, and stood back to take in the entire effect in the mirror. At the risk of stating the obvious, the effect was stunning. Glorious, in fact. But why stop with simply glorious? I decided a little more glamour was needed for the outfit—a transition to break up the monotony between the bunched-up, safety-pinned pseudo-waistband of the skirt and the plaid of the lumberjack shirt.

And that's when I had the most brilliant idea of all: a giant over-sized bow cut out of the skirt fabric and tied at my waist.

Mike drop.

It was a great day to be me as I headed to church in my black tube skirt and lumberjack shirt and giant-bow waistband and ratted-permed hair and brilliant red lipstick.

I was amazing.

Until.

Until I sat down and bent over to grab a hymnal and heard a noise that sounded suspiciously like a rip. And a pop. And another rip. From hem to glorious waistband, my perfect outfit was falling apart before my eyes.

Sigh. For a moment I had been so close.

So close to amazing.

⁓ᴘ

That's me. Always trying. Always striving. Always planning and dreaming and brilliant-ideaing. I'm the embodiment of hope spring-ing eternal. I wake up every morning with big plans and creative projects and giant mountains to climb. I'm valiantly striving to put my best foot forward every day. Sometimes I succeed beyond my wildest dreams.

And sometimes . . . not so much.

I'm the one who brings slice-and-bake cookies to a potluck. Not baked, *of course.* Only sliced. I'm the smiling guest clutching the package of cookies, still in the bright yellow wrapper. The dessert bringer who patiently explains to the hostess that it might be fun to have a hands-on activity after dinner. *Except.* Except I start talking and forget about the cookies while they're in the oven, and the cookies end up burned, and we have to go out for ice cream for dessert.

I'm the one who shows up late for praise team practice, leaping up onstage in a hurry, only to be greeted with a giant bear hug from my husband. I'm the soprano who thinks my husband is hugging me in a giant show of affection, proclaiming to the world how incredible I am. And then? I discover that he was only hugging me to grab the toilet paper off the back of my skirt.

I'm the one who moved with my husband and four children hundreds of miles across the Mississippi River, from the Dallas Metroplex to the rolling hills of Kentucky, leaving behind everything and everyone we knew and loved because we felt God's calling. That's me—following a dream without too much of a plan, let alone a safety net.

Some days I am so amazing it would make your head spin.

I'm a wife and a mother and a sister and a friend and a writer and a reader and a neighbor and a speaker and a teacher and a learner and a believer and the hula hoop champion of fourth grade and a saved daughter of the King.

I talk in conversations peppered with total asides (information that simply has to be shared, which may or may not have anything to do with the current conversation) and watch the Hallmark channel even though I know how every movie ends. I wave my hands to punctuate a point, and I love a story that ends with a hand-drawn DIY.

And other days . . . I'm so close.

I have Christmas stockings still hanging on the wall in July and mismatched tennis shoes and an eyebrow that I plucked a hole in the middle of and oddly long toes and hair with ADHD. I long for a kitchen with marble countertops, and I'm jealous of anyone who doesn't have to shop in the wide-leg boot section of the shoe store. I missed my son's amazing catch at a ball game because I was staring at my phone and slipped in the parking lot trying to make it to the 80-percent-off sale. I cry when I should laugh and laugh when I should cry, and I've melted down more times than I can count in the middle of my front hallway when life overwhelmed me.

I think that's why I write my stories and tell my tales. Just in case you're like me and you occasionally mismatch your shoes or trim your own bangs when a professional might have been a better choice. Just in case you've added too much soap to the washer and watched it overflow before your eyes. Just in case you're hoping and dreaming and trying to put one foot in front of the other but you aren't sure you're going to make it to bedtime. Just in case the reality in your life is so different from what you always hoped it would be. Just in case the road ahead is so bumpy that you can't see around the next corner. Just in case you needed someone else to tell their story first.

I'm here.

I get it.

I understand.

This book is about celebrating all that is incredible, awesome, unique, and special within all of us. It's about recognizing that perfection is completely overemphasized and overrated. It's about grace and forgiveness and learning from mistakes and rejoicing and celebrating in every victory, no matter how small. It's the story of all the times I tried so hard to do-it-myself—with a few missteps along the way. As a bonus, I'm sharing the instructions for some of my favorite do-it-yourself projects at the end of each chapter, along with the lessons I've learned and the mistakes I've made.

Won't you come along for the journey?

Embrace the you God created you to be.

And discover the amazing that was there all along.

Embrace the you
God created you
to be, and discover
the amazing that
was there all along.

Our journey begins . . .

1

leap before you look

LIFE LESSON #1

*Sometimes in the middle
of all the ordinary, something
extraordinary shows up.*

remember thinking at the time I was on some sort of supersized Christian version of *Candid Camera*.

You know.

The show where people are put into random situations with absolutely no idea someone is filming them, and in the middle of seeing a car without a driver or a person falling headfirst into a pie or movers carting off random mannequins from a store window, Allen Funt shows up with a camera crew.

Except in my daydream it was Billy Graham. Or the angel Gabriel. Take your pick.

The *Candid Camera* daydream happened as I was sitting in a newly reupholstered church pew, plucking imaginary pieces of lint from the most amazing outfit combination: an asymmetrical jean skirt topped with a peasant blouse wrapped with a knitted shrug. And the icing on the outfit cake? A pair of lace-up gladiator sandals with tiny beads that shook as I crossed and uncrossed my legs.

It was an ensemble for the ages.

My outfit and I had spent the better part of the last twenty minutes acting like we weren't listening to the sermon. It was hitting a little too close to home. I was staring at the ceiling, mentally redesigning the banners hanging over the organ to resemble Gothic architecture and wondering if blue carpet was the best decor choice for the sanctuary.

But my heart?

It was listening to every word.

Our pastor was in the middle of a multipart sermon series about stepping back and letting go. For weeks he had been talking about the significance of placing God first in your life. In all things, in all ways, we are to acknowledge his sovereignty and trust him with our whole hearts. As we let go and release fear and doubt and worry and lean not on our own understanding, God will direct our paths (see Proverbs 3:5-6).

When I first read about the series in the bulletin, I almost stayed home, pulled the covers over my head, and slept in. *Why go?* I asked myself. *You're already acknowledging and trusting and releasing and leaning. You've been over all this in last year's Bible study. It's nothing new.*

I knew that Jesus was my Savior.

I had proclaimed him the Lord of my life.

I did my part at church. I helped with the choir and supported missions and sketched charts of Paul's second missionary journey and made hot dog potpie when someone was sick and planned all the Sunday school parties, complete with elaborate themes and games and a mix tape with the occasional choreographed song.

total aside

Choreography can really help break the ice at your next small group get-together. For example, "Father Abraham Had Many Sons" is an excellent choice if you want to get a party started.

The Christian boxes? I had them all checked off.

So it was with a considerable degree of reluctance that I dragged myself to church that Sunday and found myself sitting in the pew with my arms crossed, one on top of the other, bracing myself for the sermon. I was pretty sure I had heard all this before. It wasn't new to me. I had been raised in church. I had played the nonsinging innkeeper's wife in the children's Christmas pageant. I knew all the stories and parables by heart. I could recite the story of Noah and the Flood and Jonah and the whale and Jesus feeding the five thousand. I'd been first in Bible Drill as a kid. I knew where to find Malachi. I'd made woven potholders for overseas missionaries. And in a pinch, when I needed a really good Bible verse, I could quote John 3:16 standing on one foot with my eyes closed.

But this message?

To my surprise, it was different.

That day I felt like the pastor was preaching directly to me. It was as if this entire sermon series had been written in longhand, tied to a carrier pigeon, and dropped directly onto my pew. The ironic thing? The carrier pigeon had perfect timing.

For months, my husband, Denton, and I had been talking about our family's future. It all began as an off-the-cuff discussion that turned into something so much more. We'd talk and plan and dream for hours about leaving everything behind and starting fresh in a place where the green grass grew and white clouds drifted overhead in blue skies and the cows lowed and the birds chirped and the air was filled with the smell of freshly cut hay. We wanted to jump into a new adventure and begin again in a place where we could see the stars in the night sky.

Our biggest challenge was that the jump didn't involve just us. There were other hearts to consider.

At ten, our oldest, Denton Jr., was a state capital expert, a reluctant soccer player, and captain of the neighborhood kickball games. He had come into this world bubbling over with joy. By the time he was two, he had twinkling brown eyes like his dad and an irresistible toothless grin. By the time he was three, he knew that Reykjavík is the capital of Iceland and that Czechoslovakia isn't a country anymore and that the state fish of Hawaii is the humuhumunukunukuapua'a.

I'd dress him up in yard-sale overalls with a big plaid pocket in the front, tiny hiking boots, and a faded jean jacket with his name scrawled across the back. Then I'd perch him in the front of a Target shopping cart. We didn't have a dime to our name, so we window-shopped. With him in his overalls and me in my stirrup pants, we strolled down aisle after aisle of the store. He'd cheerfully peer out from under the brim of his baseball cap and wave at the other shoppers. They'd wave back, smile at me, and whisper to each other how cute he was.

I'd beam with pride and tell myself what an incredible mother I was. I'd look at this tiny human, sitting so politely in the shopping cart seat sharing his state-fish knowledge with anyone who would listen, and mentally pat myself on the back. It was official.

I was amazing.

Maybe I should write parenting books, I told myself. *Maybe I should teach classes to other moms. Why hide my light under a bushel when I am obviously so successful in the mother department?*

I lived in that self-congratulatory haze for three years.

Delusion was wonderful.

Until.

Until our next son came along.

Three years later, Zachary arrived on a wintry day in December, grabbing life by the tail and never letting go. He was mischievous and lively and energetic, and he never met a mountain he didn't want to climb. He represented. He stood up and was counted. His curiosity was boundless, and he devoured books like they were candy and believed that one day dinosaurs would rule the earth again. He bounced and giggled and rolled and skateboarded his way into our hearts, but he never, ever sat still in the seat of the red Target cart.

He peeled gum off the floor of the store instead.

And then? We thought we were done. We thought our family was complete. We were blessed with two boys who kept us on our toes and filled our lives to the brim with energy and enthusiasm. It was time to pack up the strollers and the burp cloths and the tiny mobile with the elephant that beeped. Then, on the brink of trading it all in for a basketball hoop, we discovered I was pregnant again.

With twins.

It was a challenging pregnancy. I contracted fifth disease in the first trimester, and at twenty-four weeks the twins were diagnosed with a condition that sometimes affects identical twins called twin-to-twin transfusion syndrome. I spent over four weeks in the hospital on bed rest so the nursing staff could monitor the babies for signs of distress. At twenty-nine weeks, the situation became serious, and the doctors were forced to operate. Almost three months before their due date, I gave birth to tiny, premature twin girls weighing in at just over two pounds each.

Now our twin girls, Westleigh and Whitney, were four and full of sugar and spice. They were professional Sharpie wall-drawers and hostesses for tea parties, which they served to monkeys and elephants with giggles and laughter.

Westleigh Anne was born a minute before her sister and lived up to every letter of her name. She was an Anne, a tradition in our family. The oldest girl of the oldest girl was always an Anne, just like me and my mother and my grandmother before her. We Annes are known for our tenacity, inner strength, and ability to speak our minds, and she was no exception.

Her sister, Whitney, was the littlest of my children. The youngest. The tiniest basketball player with the biggest heart. She was the curly-haired tumbler, the dancer, the cartwheeler, the Scripture memorizer, and her sister's biggest cheerleader. And she never met a stray she didn't want to bring home and name after someone from the Bible.

For our children, Texas was home. It's where their school was, where their church was, where their friends were. And perhaps most of all, where they had grown up surrounded by a large extended family. A family who had attended every birthday, every muddy soccer game, every crowded school open house, and every school play where someone dressed up as a giant block of cheese.

Leaving would be a big adjustment.

After all, we'd grown up in Texas. It was all we knew. My husband was a pharmacist who worked for a nonprofit foundation in downtown Dallas. I ran a preschool at our local church. Our parents lived nearby. My brother and sister-in-law lived down the street in a part of town where everyone knew your name. There were aunts and cousins and grandparents and parents who were on speed dial for babysitting or broken washing machines or leaking ceilings. There was always a helping hand extended or a shoulder to cry on or an inside joke to share.

Or some combination thereof.

We lived in a historic home we'd bought four years earlier. We'd completely renovated it, with a new bathroom and an inlaid kitchen floor so beautiful you'd say grace over it. It had twenty-one closets, four bedrooms, a tiny room just for the mail, and a backyard with room for a bicycle path.

The house was wonderful. Life was wonderful. Why would we ever want to move?

But somehow the word *jump* wiggled its way into our conversations.

Our hearts wanted to move. Denton and I had both lived in small towns when we were growing up, and we wanted that for our children, too. Denton had an hour-and-a-half commute each way, and he wanted a five-minute drive in the country instead. I wanted to garden and grow corn and wear aprons and walk in the back meadow with leaves crunching under my feet. We wanted our children to live without designer labels and cell phones and learn how to climb trees and fish in the creek.

At first we just talked about jumping at random times, in random places. We talked about moving to the country and what our house would look like and how I'd always wanted to own a goat. I remember having an entire discussion while waiting in line at Chuck E. Cheese's about what type of business we would open if we moved.

But that's all it was: a discussion.

Just a distant dream.

At the time, it didn't even seem like a remote possibility. There were too many obstacles, too many complications. And the questions were endless. *How can we leave everything we know? What will we do to support ourselves? Aren't we adults? Shouldn't we be responsible and make responsible decisions? Isn't the smell of hay slightly overrated?*

Would we even remember to look up and see the stars?

But slowly, as dreams sometimes do, this dream began to grow legs and take shape over the next few months. We found several business possibilities that looked like a good fit and narrowed our options down to certain areas of the country where we thought we could live. Arkansas and Oklahoma and Tennessee all made the cut. Each of these states offered a lower cost of living with acres of beautiful countryside and a business-friendly atmosphere. We discussed our financial picture and what we should list our house for to make the whole move work.

There were moments when I remember thinking, *This is it. Today is the day. We're going to do it. Tell Pa to get the covered wagon and pack the quilts and the washboard. We are leaving it all behind and heading west.*

We traveled up to Oklahoma and looked at a pharmacy we heard might be for sale. The area was beautiful, and the small town was perfect, with a main street right out of a movie. The gas station had the perfect mix of Diet Coke with tiny, crunchy ice. But we couldn't make the finances work. Other opportunities seemed too good to be true, or we were there too late, or something just didn't feel right.

It was an exhausting roller coaster.

In the end, nothing ever seemed to happen. There was always some overwhelming obstacle in our way or a decision that didn't feel right, and we never got farther than the front door.

At my niece's birthday party one year, between the chocolate cake and the "Happy Birthday" *cha cha cha*s, I brought up the subject of moving.

"I heard about a house for sale in Kentucky," I tossed nonchalantly into conversation. "The cost of living is so much cheaper there, and I've always wanted to learn to ride a horse."

"A horse? Really?" my mother snorted. My dad grinned across the balloon arch. My brother rolled his eyes and cut another piece of cake. And me? I gazed off into the distance, as if willing the country-side to come to my front door.

total aside

If I had a horse, I would go all old school and name her Trixie. I would also try to drop Trixie's name into conversation whenever possible. Horses are great conversation starters.

Most of the time no one listened to us when we talked about moving. They'd glance at each other when we started in on our plans to jump, and they'd roll their eyes. We talked about it so much and for so long that no one really took us seriously anymore.

Truthfully? Maybe all we wanted to do was talk. And dream. And talk a little more. I'm not sure if either Denton or I thought we would actually do it. All I know is that if one day moving trucks pulled up to the house, I would have been the first one clinging to the columns on the front porch.

And then something happened that changed everything.

In the middle of all that talking and pontificating and waiting for the day we would pack up the covered wagon, an actual business proposal showed up. An independent pharmacy became available in a small town in Kentucky, and the owners wanted to know if we were interested in buying it. My husband would run the pharmacy, and I could manage the gift store.

It sounded like it might work. It sounded like a real possibility. But we had been sure before, too. Our hopes had been dashed over and over again. So with great trepidation, mixed with an extra helping of excitement, we packed our bags and headed to Kentucky for a visit.

We didn't mention our reconnaissance mission to our family. They had already heard it all before and probably wouldn't believe us anyway. Besides, it was time for a little less talk and a little more action. So, Denton and I packed our overnight bags into our minivan and headed toward the Bluegrass State.

We drove into town with a healthy dose of skepticism and our loopholes and excuses and reasons ready.

"Only an hour," we said to each other. "That's all we'll need. It's probably not even a good fit." But our hour turned into an afternoon, and our skepticism turned into hope, and our journey turned into a destination.

It was the perfect situation.

The pharmacy was a thriving business located in a small town at the edge of where the Ohio and Cumberland Rivers meet. The town had a rich history and a century-old courthouse and the remains of an inn where famous dignitaries had stayed. There was also a Civil War site and a bridge named after Thomas Jefferson's sister on the edge of town. The schools were good, and we found yummy pizza with extra toppings for only five dollars on Tuesdays at the gas station.

And the best part?

In the entire county where the pharmacy was located, there were no stoplights. Not a single one. The county did have two blinking yellow lights, even though one of them was broken. There were stop signs and deer crossing signs and congested area signs at the street corner where the old grocery store used to be.

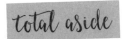

If you're wondering why it's necessary for me to point out all the roadside bells and whistles, I just wanted to make it clear that all the signs were there. Literally.

After meeting with the owner of the pharmacy, my husband and I stood on the bank of the river and gazed at the clouds drifting by in the sky. We watched as tiny branches waved to and fro in the wind.

Neither of us spoke. It all just felt so right.

We turned and headed back to Texas with our heads in the clouds.

But before we crossed the Tennessee border, doubt started to creep in. We debated the pros and cons of a momentous decision like this one. Our discussion centered mostly on the cons.

We didn't have enough money.

It was so far away.

We didn't know anyone in the town.

The real estate market for buying and selling was almost nonexistent.

We would be leaving our family.

By the time we left Tennessee and crossed into Arkansas, we'd talked ourselves out of the plan. We decided to table it until later. And by later, I think we meant never. It was a decision to be filed away and marked with a label of *someday*.

God has been
there all along.
Waiting.
Inviting us to
pause and listen.

I thought that was the end of the dream.

Until.

Until the next Sunday, when I sat in church listening in disbelief and wondering if Billy Graham and a camera crew were right around the corner. Because the sermon I was trying so hard not to listen to was entitled "Jump."

God has a sense of humor.

Jump.

Four little letters that swirled in circles, leaped off the overhead screen, spun around and around and around in my brain, and twisted me all up inside. And right there, in the middle of the sermon, in the middle of church, as I sat trembling in my peasant blouse and beaded gladiator sandals, an incredible, sovereign, powerful God was trying to get my attention. And all I could do was shake my head.

Jump.

I can't jump, I said silently. *I have a husband and a family and friends and responsibilities and a house with a big mortgage, and I'm going to give the speech at the end-of-the-year program at school. And I finally found the perfect person to highlight my hair.*

Jump.

Why me? I wondered. *What about the people two pews over? They look like jumpers. Why not stop by their pew and talk to them instead?*

Jump.

I'm scared, I mouthed. *Where will we get the money for the move, and how will we support our family, and what if we don't fit in, and what if I'm not strong enough, and what if we fail?*

Trust in me. Lean not on your own understanding. I will make your paths straight.

At last I understood. I didn't have to do this alone.

I had spent months and months searching and making lists of pros and cons and trying to decide everything all on my own. I hadn't been seeking guidance or reaching out and leaning on someone who knew me better than I knew myself.

He had been there all along. Waiting. Inviting me to pause and listen.

An incredible feeling of peace washed over me. I glanced over at my husband, who was sitting next to me, and met his gaze. He looked at me with love and compassion and a newly awakened understanding and reached for my hand. As his fingers closed quietly over mine, I could feel his heart pulsing through his fingertips. The sermon had spoken to him, too, and I could see his decision in his eyes.

Jumping wasn't going to be easy—I knew that. There were so many unanswered questions. There were dozens of difficult choices and challenges and good-byes that peppered the road ahead. A giant chasm full of bends and twists and turns lay before us.

But that morning, sitting in church redesigning banners with the debatable blue carpet under my feet, I knew the bridge had been built for our journey. God had been preparing the way all along. And so, right then and there, with the words of the sermon ringing in our ears, we jumped.

I sure hope Billy got it all on tape.

The "Just Jump" Wooden Sign

SUPPLIES

- saw
- 1 piece plywood
  (4 feet by 8 feet)
- paintbrush
- 1 quart white latex primer
- 1 bottle white acrylic paint
- printer
- several sheets printer paper
- pencil
- 1 piece graphite paper
- 1 bottle black acrylic paint
- 1 piece 100-grit sandpaper
- 1 quart satin top coat

 Cut the piece of plywood to 2 feet by 5 feet.

 Paint one coat of primer onto the plywood, and let it dry.

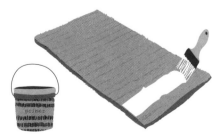

3 Paint one coat of the white paint onto the plywood, and let it dry. Paint a second coat of white paint onto the plywood, and let it dry.

4 Choose a font for the words "Just Jump," and size the letters to fit the sign. The letters should be approximately 12 inches high. Print the letters out on your printer.

5 Trace the letters onto the plywood using a pencil and graphite paper.

6 Remove the graphite paper, and fill in the traced outline with two coats of black paint, allowing each coat to dry fully.

7 Sand the sign lightly to distress it. Seal the finished sign with the satin top coat, and let it dry.

8 Hang up the sign as a reminder that even though jumping can be scary, it gets easier after the first leap.

2

knock, knock; who's there?

LIFE LESSON #2

*Into every life a little
wet paint must fall.*

I remember reading somewhere that after expending the incredible amount of mental energy needed to make a big decision, it's always a good idea to pause. Slow down. Put on your thinking cap. Walk instead of run. Smell the proverbial flowers. Maybe pour a cup of coffee and make a list and take a moment to plan the next steps of your journey.

That sounds like amazingly sound advice.

On paper.

This is the kind of unsolicited advice I give others. It's the kind of advice they hand out in Hallmark movies when the girl arrives back in her hometown, tired and weary and disillusioned after her film career didn't work out, and she wants to open up a bed-and-breakfast with the inheritance left to her by her grandmother. Right on cue, she runs into her high school boyfriend at the coffee shop, and he's full of sage insights and astute suggestions about taking life at a slower pace even though he hasn't seen her in ten years. She heeds his pearls of wisdom, presses pause, slows down, and listens to her heart, and then they walk off into the sunset and happily-ever-after.

That is exactly the kind of world-changing, dream-creating, bed-and-breakfast-making advice I'm talking about.

Except.

Except I didn't ever try to make it in Hollywood. I can't cook breakfast. I think walking off into the sunset is a little overrated sometimes, and I rarely, if ever, listen to anyone else's words of wisdom.

Even when I should.

So instead of pausing and thinking and planning where we were going from here, I painted. After all, we needed to sell our house, and I'm almost positive I read somewhere that house selling should involve a little less talk and a little more action.

total aside

Hallmark movies, along with Schoolhouse Rock! and Saved by the Bell, are all excellent sources of reliable life lessons. I refer to them frequently when making difficult decisions.

To say I painted a few things that next month is like saying *90210* is just a zip code. I was on a mission to paint anything that didn't move. I painted cabinets and door moldings and crown moldings and floor moldings and hallways and rooms. I painted as fast as my brush would let me.

I painted the kitchen and the lower cabinets and the neglected piece of molding everyone always forgets about behind the refrigerator. I painted the front door and the windows on either side of the entry and the numbers on the house. I painted the shelves in the pantry and the back wall of the closet, and just when I thought there was nothing left to paint, I went all Van Gogh on the reverse side of a piece of linoleum and painted a floorcloth.

It was as if with every swipe, I was painting away my looming decisions. As I frenetically painted the molding in the twins' room with my messy bun bobbing up and down, wondering whether crayon marks could pass for decorative art and itching the end of my nose with paint-covered fingers, I saw it.

A car driving slowly past the window near the side of the house.

I stood frozen, mid-itch, staring at the vehicle outside the window. I'm not even sure why I paused. I don't know what it was about that particular car at that particular moment that caught my undivided, paint-splattered attention.

But I knew.

I knew it as surely as you know that a really good bobby pin makes for a good hair day and that putting your hand on your waist makes you look skinnier in pictures and that red lipstick makes the world a better place.

I knew that I knew that I knew.

Those were our people.

Those were the people we were unaware we'd been looking for. The people in that car—the wonderful, incredible family driving by at a snail's pace? I knew they were going to buy our house. Visions of packing up the house and handing them the keys and leaving on a jet plane danced inside my head.

I put down my paintbrush and braced myself for what the future held. The roller coaster had officially left the station. This was the moment. This was the first step in our jumping journey.

I stood up, straightened my T-shirt, twisted my hair in a vain attempt to un-messy my messy bun, and tried unsuccessfully to wipe paint off the tips of my shaking fingers. I was ready. This was it.

It was time to meet my destiny.

Instead, I watched in disbelief as the car slowly drove away. *What?* Where were they going? Why were they leaving?

I ran to the window and flattened my nose against it. In despair, I reached out my fingers in the direction of the departing car. Didn't they know? Didn't they understand? Hadn't they been cc'd on the same memo I'd gotten? They were supposed to stop and walk up the winding sidewalk, past the boxwood bushes and wrought-iron urns. They were supposed to make their way up the brick steps and reach for the monogrammed brass door knocker.

And knock.

I was pretty sure all of that was somewhere in the script.

As I stared at the retreating taillights, my messy bun wilted.

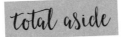

It's important to note that a messy bun is an excellent choice for third-day hair when you are late for an appointment or forget you are in charge of something super important like the St. Patrick's Day party at school. Add yoga pants, and people might think you've been working out.

Dejectedly, I turned away from the window and headed back to finish painting the room. A forlorn sigh escaped from my lips as I jabbed the paintbrush into the white paint, swiped at the molding, and watched as the paint slowly dripped onto the drop cloth. Then, as if in slow motion, a few drops escaped over the edge of the base molding and drizzled onto the floor.

Drip. Drop. Drip.

I'd better clean up that paint, I thought. *Even though it doesn't matter. Even though the car didn't stop. Even though my gut instinct was wrong.*

I sighed again, put down the paintbrush, and reached for a roll of paper towels to clean up the mess. I ripped off a sheet and began scrubbing at the drops of paint on the antique wood flooring. But no matter how hard I scrubbed the floor, the paint drops refused to come off.

I started to sob. And scrub. And sob some more.

Giant tears dripped off the edge of my nose, mixing in with the paint on the floor. All this busy. All this action. All this painting.

For what?

Hadn't I listened to God's vision for my life? Wasn't I acting according to his plan? Weren't we following the call and packing our bags and going all Israelite and heading to the Promised Land?

"I'm here!" I shouted to the empty room between sobs. "I'm listening. I'm painting every room in this house. I'm trying. What more do you want from me? Don't you see how hard I'm working? Don't you see my commitment? Why did you bring that car by the house only to have it drive away? Seriously, God?" I wailed.

I sounded like a four-year-old who just discovered her favorite toy has been snatched away. But I didn't care. I was justified. I had every reason to be upset. I was right.

Or was I?

The thought came out of nowhere, stopping me in my tracks.

Was I right? Or was I so busy with my plans and my schedule and my overzealous painting that somewhere along the way I'd completely lost sight of what was truly important? Was selling a house so difficult for God that he needed that particular car with those particular people? Did the God who formed the heavens and the earth and the universe and all of creation really need me to paint the house to sell it? Was my faith so small that I believed God needed my assistance? Calling all mustard seeds. I seemed to have misplaced mine.

total aside

Once I saw a necklace made from a mustard seed encased in resin. It was beautiful and super small. So small, in fact, that I had to squint to see it. And of course all that smallness proves the point of the entire parable.

"Enough," I said, putting down the paper towel. "Enough painting. Enough action. Enough frantic activity. Enough of what *I* want. Enough trying to make this happen on my terms and my schedule."

Let it go, I sensed my heart telling me. *Simply let it go.*

And so, I did.

Right then and there, I let all the busy go, and I felt the burden being lifted off my shoulders. In an instant, the weight of a thousand decisions was gone. My heart felt as light as the bristles of my paintbrushes.

With a feeling of peace, I started packing up all the painting supplies. I returned the ladder to the garage and carefully folded up the drop cloths and put the paintbrushes in the sink and went to search Pinterest for ways to get paint off a wood floor. Then, as I was walking to the computer, I glanced out the window and saw it again.

The same car.

And once again, it was driving by at a snail's pace. I shut my eyes.

I couldn't look. I didn't want to follow where the car turned or see if it stopped or worry about where it was going.

I was done with doing it my way. I wasn't going to pin any hopes on that car. I wasn't going to fret or wring my hands or agonize. I wasn't going to try to make anything happen.

This time, I was simply going to trust.

I reached up and shut the curtains to sever any and all car communication and then continued my Pinterest search. My fingers flew across the keyboard as I typed in H-O-W T-O G-E-T P-A . . . but before I ever reached I-N-T, I heard a knock at the door.

I wish I could tell you I ran and threw it open. But I didn't.

Isn't it funny that when we're faced with what we've been hoping and dreaming and praying for, we are so often reluctant to take what's right in front of us? Instead of reaching for the dream, I stood frozen in the hallway with one thought running through my head: *Do I have paint on my forehead?*

Then it came again. Another knock. I inched toward the door and finally answered it.

Standing there was the young couple I had seen in the car. They looked at me sheepishly, shrugging their shoulders almost in unison. They shot each other a nervous glance and then spoke the sweetest words I've ever heard.

"Hi. Someone from church mentioned you might want to sell your house, and we were just driving by and would love to look at it. Are you still thinking about selling?"

This was God—I was sure of it this time. This was the almighty Creator of the heavens and the earth performing a miracle.

There was no sign in the yard. We didn't have a real estate agent.

I let all the busy go,
and I felt the
burden being lifted off
my shoulders.
My heart felt as
light as the bristles
of my paintbrushes.

We had told only a few people we were thinking about moving. We didn't list it online or post it on Craigslist or put it on Facebook.

In the end, none of that was necessary. It was becoming even more evident to me that this jump was God ordained.

I invited the couple in and sent a silent prayer toward heaven that the house was relatively picked up (aside from the collection of ground-in Cheerios on the kitchen floor, Thomas the Train running through the hallway, and the cans of paint scattered across the back bedroom).

The couple walked in and peered into the entryway with its freshly painted stripes, and I offered to take them on a tour. I walked them through room after room: the living room, the family room, and the study.

total aside

If you are selling a house and have a room that needs a little pick-me-up, painting stripes is a cost-effective way to create visual interest in a space without breaking the bank. Just as with clothes, vertical stripes have a flattering effect.

Right around the time we were touring the back porch, with its outdoor fireplace and hand-painted diamond squares on the floor, I looked over and noticed the couple nodding and smiling and glancing at each other. I could see it in their eyes: they had fallen in love with the house.

After we'd finished the tour, we sat in the living room and talked about our families. Denton and I told them about the jump and the sermon we'd listened to and the business opportunity that had presented itself in Kentucky and how we felt like this was what God had intended for us in the next chapter of our lives.

This was our journey.

Over sweet tea and conversation, they asked us how much we wanted for the house. We gave them a number that would allow us to pay off our mortgage and still have enough left for a down payment on the pharmacy. And then we held our breath and waited.

The decision took only a moment. They glanced at each other and looked at us. Without hesitation, they announced they would take it.

"How quickly do you want to close?" they asked.

From there, the rest of the details are fuzzy. I vaguely remember talking about dates and inspections and listing the improvements we'd made to the house and offering to sell them some of our furniture. But there was one detail that stood out in particular.

Just as they were leaving, I apologized for the mess and explained that I was working on painting the rooms and the moldings.

"Just overlook all of this," I said. "The mess will be completely cleaned up. Everything will be freshly painted before you move in," I assured them.

"Oh, don't worry about the paint," the wife said with a smile. "I'm going a little different direction. I'm already planning to have everything repainted in new colors that match our decor."

I think I heard God laughing.

Let-It-Go Curtain Rods

- saw
- 1 raw wood dowel rod
  (½ inch thick, 36 inches long)
- 4 raw wood finials with
  mounting screws
- 4 raw wood brackets

- paintbrush
- 1 quart white latex primer
- 1 quart white latex paint
- electric drill
- screws

1. Cut the dowel rod into two 18-inch long pieces.

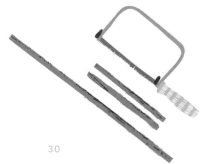

2. Paint one coat of primer onto the dowel rod pieces, wood finials, and wood brackets, and let them dry.

3 Paint one coat of white paint onto the dowel rod pieces, wood finials, and wood brackets, and let them dry. Then, paint a second coat, and let them dry completely.

4 Drill a hole into each end of the dowel rod pieces, matching the width of the mounting screws on the finials.

5 Attach one bracket with screws 5 inches out from the left edge of the window and 2 inches above the window. Attach a second bracket 18 inches to the right of this first bracket. Repeat for the right corner of the window.

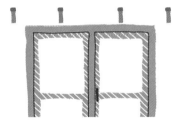

6 Hang the curtains on the dowel rods. Screw the finials into the previously drilled holes.

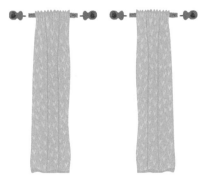

7 Place the dowel rods with curtains and finials into the brackets on each side of the window. Fluff the curtains.

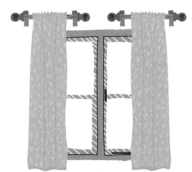

8 When dark, gloomy clouds gather outside your window and doubt and fear creep in, reach up to close the curtains against the sleet and the hail and the wind and the rain, and rely on God to help you weather the storm.

3

*I would move
six hundred miles*

LIFE LESSON #3

*True beauty is often just below
the surface. You just have
to scrub a little to see it.*

Memories bounced off the ceilings and the floors of the empty house as I made my last pilgrimage through the hallways. That morning my mission was single minded: to tell our almost-forever home that parting was such sweet sorrow. The moving trucks were packed, and the overloaded minivan was parked in the driveway.

It was time for us to say good-bye, the house and me.

I could almost hear it mourning with me as I walked from room to room, sharing a farewell of epic proportions.

Remember the scene in *Gone with the Wind* when Scarlett wanders through the night and ends up standing in the field at sunrise? She's hungry and tired, with a haunting beauty about her, streaks of dirt on her face, and an incredibly wild hairdo. She's sobbing and grabbing dirt and missing Tara, and then her hunger drives her to randomly start digging up a carrot. As she stands there with tears streaming down her dirt-streaked face, she raises her fist to the sky. The music builds in a perfect crescendo, and she declares with every fiber of her being, "As God is my witness, they're not going to lick me. I'm going to live through this, and when it's all over, I'll never be hungry again."

And . . . scene.

Saying good-bye was almost as dramatic as that.

With heavy shoulders, I told the living room farewell and mentioned to the family room that it had better check on the back porch occasionally and wished the kitchen happiness and reminded the bathroom that it needed air freshener. With that I turned and waved to the empty room and locked the door.

One chapter finished. Another just beginning.

It was an easy trip to our new home. We traveled across Arkansas; turned left at Tennessee; drove past a horse barn, miles of white picket fence, a chicken barn, and forty-seven cow pastures; and arrived at our destination at the end of a winding country road. Fortified by four giant Diet Cokes and three fast-food stops, we rolled into town with four children, two moving vans, a dog, and a Styrofoam cup full of optimism.

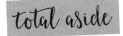

Optimism is the one thing you should pack when you leave everything you hold dear to travel across the country in an overloaded minivan and a Diet Coke haze to follow a dream. You might also include sunglasses to block out any cross-country eye rolls.

Still holding on to skepticism with one hand, we didn't want to buy a house immediately. Instead, our plan was to rent a place while we looked for the home of our dreams. We chose a small house whose key selling point lay in the fact that the washer was located in the kitchen while the dryer was hooked up in the family room, several rooms away. Besides the obvious benefit of additional exercise between loads, you could watch your clothes dry and *Jeopardy* all at the same time.

It was here that we landed.

This was going to be our new temporary home.

That night we ate dinner at a card table, rolled out some sleeping bags, and alternated between looking at each other as if to say, "What have we done?" and having random fits of giggles as if to say, "Look what we did!"

We drifted off to sleep with visions of farmhouses and winding country roads and twinkling stars dancing in our heads.

In the morning, the unpacking began.

We opened the doors to the moving vans and started with the largest pieces first. We unpacked the beds and the couch and the chairs and the dining room set and a giant wooden sign that was slightly oversized for the space. Next, we unloaded the mattresses and the leather chairs and an oversized chalkboard and a lamp resembling an oddly shaped pineapple. Finally, we unloaded the table.

This wasn't just any table.

It was a table of magnificent proportions—with a story to tell. My mother had purchased it years ago at a yard sale and then decided it needed too much work and was a little too wobbly and didn't really fit in her space. In a gesture of generosity, she promptly handed it down to me.

It was a family heirloom in need of a makeover.

When we first acquired the table, it was a true diamond in the rough. It was two feet wide and eight feet long, with spindly legs and molding around the top that didn't quite match. It was covered with nicks and dings, and the top had deep grooves from years of use. It had lived a lifetime before we ever met.

A lifetime full of late nights and poor fashion choices.

But it was perfect for our home in Texas. It just needed someone with a vision—and some elbow grease. I started the table makeover with the top. I sanded and refinished the entire surface so the original wood shone. I intended to refinish the legs as well, but there were too many grooves and nicks that I couldn't sand, so I decided to paint them instead.

Painting the legs proved to be an indecisive journey. First, I painted the legs blue, and then I changed my mind and painted them black. *Something just isn't right*, I told myself. Then I changed my mind again and painted the legs red.

But it still wasn't working.

Maybe I need to go simpler, I thought. Impatiently, I scrapped the whole red and blue and black thing and painted the legs white. *Better*, I thought. *Much better*. I reached for the sandpaper, scolding myself for my indecision and my unfortunate previous color choices, and started to distress the table's legs.

At that moment, something incredible happened.

The more I sanded, the more amazing the finish became. Distressing the piece revealed layer upon layer of different colors under the white top coat. In some places, you could see hints of blue, and in other spots red and black peeked through the edges of the finish. Emboldened, I sanded harder and harder until the original wood finish mixed in with the layers of colors.

And somehow it all worked. I added a layer of stain and then protected the finish with a final coat of sealant. When I was done, I could hear the faint strains of the "Hallelujah" chorus winging their way from heaven.

I repurposed it as a desk and paired it with vintage English school chairs with woven cane seats. I lined up locker bins on the tabletop for books and papers and hung a train station clock over the table. To finish off the display, I stacked tattered encyclopedias and baskets of antique maps next to the edge of the desk.

The table was a showpiece.

Whenever people stopped by for a visit, they commented on that table. Accolades poured in from far and wide. It was enough to make a table's head spin.

"Wow," they'd say. "That is some table." And my personal favorite line: "They sure don't make tables like that anymore."

My table and I would beam with pride and show off our legs and humble-brag about our painted coat of many colors. We'd silently tell ourselves how amazing we were and high-five each other after the guests left.

After traveling halfway across the country, the table arrived in Kentucky with us. My heart raced when the movers unpacked it and carried it down the ramp. It was like having one of my people right here with me in the Bluegrass State. I placed it against the wall in the living room and sighed.

It was time to get settled in our new home, my table and me.

⌒ꞁꝋ

The next couple of weeks were a flurry of activity. We unpacked boxes and visited churches and enrolled the kids in school and discovered that the closest Walmart was 22.1 miles away and that it snows in Kentucky.

I met some of our neighbors, and someone brought over fried chicken, and I started decorating our new house. Everything was slowly falling into place. Even the washer and dryer got along well together despite their awkward locations. I put up new curtains and hung art in the hallway and sewed a tablecloth and painted a stool.

When the last picture was in place, I looked around and decided it was time to have a party. You know. A party to introduce my new house to the neighborhood.

And my table? It was going to be the guest of honor at the festivities. I couldn't wait to show it off, even though I was a little nervous about inviting some new people we had met at church and school and the dollar store. I crossed my fingers and hoped people would actually show up.

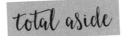

It's a proven fact that red lipstick can provide confidence in difficult situations like a gathering in a new town or meeting your in-laws for the first time or even your first Pampered Chef party. When applying, just make sure you avoid your teeth.

When the day of the party arrived, everything was ready. I had printed *Welcome* in bright red letters on a burlap banner, and I stacked cupcakes from a local bakery on a silver platter. The kitchen island was set with a pitcher of sweet tea and a giant milk glass bowl full of punch. I finished off the party decor by sprinkling tiny flowers and hearts and framed quotes with encouraging words all over the top of the island.

And me? I was dressed in the perfect outfit for the occasion. I layered a sweater over a lace top and leggings and wore tiny ballet flats with a flower on each one that twinkled when I walked. I teased up my hair and added a bobby pin, and then I put on a giant pair of sparkly earrings. I finished my ensemble with a coat of red lipstick.

It was my first party in my new adopted town. I couldn't wait. My earrings trembled in anticipation.

The doorbell rang, and I ran to welcome my new friends into the house. They streamed into the living room, bringing housewarming gifts like hand soap and a potted plant and a new package of coffee. We laughed and talked and joked like we were old friends, and while we munched on cupcakes and sipped sweet tea, I gave them a tour of the house. We went through the living room and the family room and saw the giant wooden sign and the kitchen washer. And then, at last, we arrived at the table.

I paused in front of my masterpiece and waited.

I waited for the accolades. I waited for the oohs and ahhs and the wistful sighs. I listened for the "Where did you get that?" and the "How did you make it?" and the ever-popular "I wish I were lucky enough to have a table like that."

Instead, there was only silence.

I cleared my throat and kind of tilted my head toward the table encouragingly. *Maybe they just need an opening to start a conversation,* I thought. *Maybe they're simply speechless when confronted with an item of such incredible artistic beauty. Or maybe they're too nervous to ask me about the table. After all, we haven't known each other that long.*

I offered what I thought was an inviting smile and, with a hand wave worthy of Vanna on *Wheel of Fortune*, gestured toward the table. My new friends looked at the table and then looked at me. They exchanged awkward smiles and asked if the table had come from a yard sale and then promptly turned back to their sweet tea.

Hello? Anyone? Anyone notice an amazing table here?

Still, no one spoke.

Shrugging my shoulders, I continued the tour with great fanfare and turned into another room to point out our antique bed, which had been handed down through the generations on my husband's side of the family. As the other ladies filed down the hallway, one of my guests pulled me aside.

"Can I ask you a question?" she said in a stage whisper.

"Of course!" I smiled. "Ask me anything."

"You see—" She stopped midsentence and then glanced around the room as if at a loss for words. "I was thinking . . ." She glanced nervously at me.

"Yes?"

"I love your new home and all," she said. "It's decorated so pretty, and I love how you put everything together. I just had a quick question about the table."

I brightened. *Ahhh. The table,* I thought. This was a familiar subject. *I'm glad someone finally noticed!*

I turned to her with a grin. "I'd love to talk about the table. Did you have something specific you wanted to discuss?"

She walked into the living room and patted the top of the table. "I was thinking," she said. "I love the size and shape of it, and I know it came from a yard sale, and you probably haven't had a chance to paint the legs yet. So, in the meantime, I have an extra tablecloth if you want to borrow it."

I stood speechless, unable to form a coherent sentence. All I could think was, *Does she mean my table?*

A tablecloth?

A tablecloth for my Hallelujah table?

I smiled weakly in her direction, thanked her for her generous offer, and mumbled something about needing to check on the other guests. Then I promptly walked over to the refreshment table, grabbed a cup of punch, and guzzled it like it was the last cup of water on a desert island. With that I plastered a *Knots Landing* smile on my face and returned to the party.

But on the inside? I wasn't smiling. Not even a little. I went all Lesley Gore and gathered my tattered pride around me and told myself that it was my party and I could cry if I wanted to.

I was stunned.

total aside

This is the part of the story where you probably notice I was having a pity party for myself in the middle of an actual party. I get it. The irony is not lost on me, either.

I felt rejected and lonely and sad, with a bruised ego that would make a month-old banana look good. What was I doing here? Why had we moved here? These people didn't get me. They didn't understand me or my table. I thought they would appreciate something new. Something different. Something unique and one of a kind.

But instead?

It was like fitting a square table leg into a round hole.

Maybe this whole dream wasn't going to work out after all.

The festivities drew to a close, and one by one the guests left amid waves and hugs and promises to get together. Eventually, I was the only one left standing in my kitchen, with just cupcake crumbs and the sagging welcome banner and dozens of empty punch cups for company.

I tried so hard, I thought. *And I'm exhausted from trying. I'm not going to do this anymore. I'm done. I'm packing up the moving vans, setting the GPS for home, and returning to my people with my tail between my legs. Everyone will understand. After all, I really did try.*

And then the tiniest of voices whispered to my heart.

Or did you? Did you try to fit in and learn more about your new friends, or did you simply set out to impress? Did you invite them into your home to make them feel welcome, or did you want to show them how you aren't really from here, because truthfully, somewhere inside of you, you think you're better?

Truth.

Heart check.

And in the silence of the room, even the table was raising its eyebrows at me.

Somehow, I had gotten mixed up along the way. I thought I was jumping to a new place to bring cutting-edge ideas and red lipstick and giant earrings and sparkly shoes and giant wooden signs and fancy table makeovers to a place that might not have seen anything like them before. I thought I was there to change them.

I was wrong.

My new friends had shown me true friendship. They demonstrated

We were here
for the lessons
we were going
to learn.

generosity of spirit and kindness and encouragement to a new member of their community. They welcomed me and showered me with gifts and smiles and hugs, but I hadn't really paid attention. I had overlooked all the welcome in my grand attempt to impress.

In that moment, I took a look at my own heart and found it wanting. All along I had been thinking an almighty God had called us to this place and this town at this time in our lives for the lessons we were going to teach.

In reality, we were here for the lessons we were going to learn.

I gathered up the punch cups, placed them in the sink, and started to clean up the mess from the party. Humming quietly to myself, I glanced across the room at my new window treatments. "I have so much to learn," I thought aloud. "No worries," I told myself. "If things get a little rocky, I'll get creative and make a new dress for myself out of the curtains."

Just like Scarlett did.

"Coat of Many Colors" Refinished Table

+ clean rag
+ 1 wooden table
  (*preferably from a yard sale*)
+ 1 package 60-grit sandpaper
+ 1 package 100-grit sandpaper
+ 1 package 120-grit sandpaper
+ tack cloth
+ foam brush
+ 1 quart wood stain

Wipe down the table to remove dirt and grime.

 Begin sanding the table with 60-grit sandpaper. Sand until the old finish is removed.

 Smooth out the wood by sanding with 100-grit sandpaper.

Complete one final sanding with 120-grit sandpaper.

Wipe down the entire table with a tack cloth to remove any dust and debris.

 Stain the table with your desired stain color. Let it dry.

7 Sand the table lightly with 100-grit sandpaper to remove any rough spots in the finish. Wipe down the table with a tack cloth to remove any dust.

8 Apply a final coat of stain.

9 Ask your newly finished table
   to cohost a neighborhood
   party with you.

4

every house needs a happily-ever-after

LIFE LESSON #4

Life isn't always like the movies; it's the rewritten script that has the best ending.

Some people are simply destined for greatness. Their path is written in the stars, glittering with a future full of awards, bright lights, and ticker-tape parades. The history books are full of their accomplishments: climbing Mount Everest or sailing the seven seas or inventing the add-a-bead necklace or finding the cure for split ends or discovering where all the extra socks go in the dryer.

Me? I was born to star in a Hallmark movie.

I was destined to live in a world where every occasion has the perfect outfit and a happily-ever-after.

It's like the girl who inherits a candy stand from her great-grandmother and travels back to her hometown to face the dilemma of whether to sell the business to the local candy monopoly or continue the family's long-standing tradition of selling fine chocolate confections shaped like local tourist attractions. She arrives in town, gets a cup of coffee, randomly meets the boy from second-period algebra class who stood her up for prom, and realizes that he never meant to break her heart. She falls in love with him over the last fifty minutes of the movie and ends up living in her great-grandmother's house selling candy for the rest of her life.

Life. It's a movie script just waiting to be written.

I started composing my first Hallmark script the day I got engaged. I was an almost-college student, and my husband was in the military. I had our entire future planned out, down to the monogrammed linen napkins. We would get married in a church with stained-glass windows, and he would wear his dress whites, and we would move into a historic two-bedroom apartment on a military base with hundred-year-old floors, industrial light fixtures, rustic cabinets, and vintage military shelving.

He would sail the seas defending our country, and I would maintain the home front in cardigans and pearls, organizing quilt parties, baking pies, mailing care packages, knitting hammocks for the soldiers, and planning welcome-home rallies. He would return from overseas to a full social calendar, complete with dances at the mess hall, dinners at the club, and lunches by the waterfront. On off nights, we would invite other military couples over for baccarat and card parties and outdoor barbecues, and we'd serve sweet tea with lime in glasses with tiny pink flamingo stir straws.

Sigh.

And my hair would flip up at the ends.

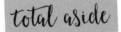

I haven't always been about a hair flip. When I was in sixth grade, I was very committed to rolling my hair under. It took hours. I'd start at the top and carefully curl it under all around my face until it looked like a jelly roll. And then I did what any good sister would do: I passed on my technique to my little sister. After all, I didn't want to be the only one with an amazing, pastry-like hairdo.

In reality, however, nothing ever lived up to the script. Life was nothing like the movies. I discovered that hammocks weren't really a thing on base, and when friends came over, we ordered pizza and watched movies. We did go to a dance once, but it was in the middle of the street and I wore a rhinestone-studded jean jacket and a bandana on my head.

Base housing wasn't an option since the waiting list was too long, so instead we moved into an apartment with one room and a twin bed that doubled as a couch and a kitchen that was a little more *Land of the Lost* than *Anchors Aweigh*. My husband was called away to sea for six months at a time, and I missed him desperately. When he finally arrived home, I didn't have the slightest interest in a full social calendar. I just wanted quiet dinners with him, and I wore more prairie skirts than pearls.

And with all that gravity, my hair didn't even flip at all.

Having life go off script didn't do anything to squelch my visions of my own happily-ever-after. I just kept dreaming and hoping and waiting and writing new scripts. I kept picking up the tatters of my daydreams and forging on ahead to the next adventure. Some people might have paused. Some people might have realized that every day isn't like the movies. Some people might have realized that real life is, well, *real*.

Not me.

Not even close.

⁓ᵖ

My Hallmark channel subscription never wavered. Fourteen years into our marriage, when we were planning our move to Kentucky, I was still writing scripts in my head. Moving to the rental was the opening act,

We can make
our own plans, but
the Lord gives
the right answer.

PROVERBS 16:1, NLT

but the main show was about to start. It was time to say good-bye to the disjointed washer and dryer and find our forever home.

The script I wrote for finding our new house was straight out of a Saturday night made-for-TV movie. I dreamed of building a white clapboard farmhouse with a picket fence. It would have a wraparound front porch and a matching chicken barn, and it would overlook the river. The house would have acres and acres of farmland, where we'd grow our own wheat and harvest it every fall and grind it into flour and make fresh bread every day.

We'd have cows and horses and pigs, and we'd show our goats at the county fair and win blue ribbons and tiny brass trophies. Every weekend we'd dance at hoedowns, and I'd wear kerchiefs and giant-pocketed aprons. I'd French braid my hair and stop wearing makeup and sprout freckles on the tip of my nose.

And at night Denton and I would walk hand in hand under the stars.

The long-awaited moment had finally arrived. It was time to start searching for a piece of property to build on.

After two months of searching, we found our own little piece of the Bluegrass State. It was right outside of town, around the bend, at the bottom of a hill overlooking the river. It was three acres deep and two acres wide, and if I squinted, I could almost see the farmhouse we were going to build, with its white clapboard siding and black roof with a tiny cupola and a rooster weather vane that spun around in the wind.

It was land we could run across on a sunny day. A place where we could wiggle our toes in the grass and Hula-Hoop in the summer. There was enough land to grow and breathe and dance and cartwheel and pitch a tent and stare up at the Big Dipper in the night sky. Six whole Kentucky acres. Wonderfully, gloriously, incredibly, amazingly ours.

Just like in the script.

After we bought the land, I found house plans that matched the home of my dreams. It would be two stories with a reclaimed wood door and a living room that opened into a kitchen that opened into a dining room. There would be a laundry room with a farmhouse sink and a fireplace in the great room and floor-to-ceiling windows that overlooked the river. There would be a paneled study and ship-lap walls and a barn wood ceiling in the game room and the tiniest powder room with a vintage sink and a built-in linen closet. And the icing on top? A wraparound porch.

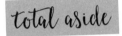

Try to say the words "barn wood ceiling" without getting a standing ovation from everyone listening. Seriously. I'm an expert at working this phrase into conversation. Everywhere. Anywhere. Fact: it's a great topic of conversation in the produce aisle at Walmart.

We hired a general contractor, talked to the bank, made sure the electricity and the water and the cable were accessible, and spent hours discussing the previously unheard-of topic of septic tanks. Finally, we were ready to begin building.

Later that week my husband called me, excitement flitting across the phone lines. "They're laying the driveway," he said. "Can you believe it? We're doing this. The rock is going down right now."

I couldn't wait. I had to see it. I drove those winding country roads and rolling hills as fast as I dared and pulled around the corner. Suddenly, there it was. Just past the bend on the far side of the property was the first tangible sign of our dream house. The driveway was only a few yards long, and it was rocky and dusty at the moment, but it was undeniably, unmistakably, unbelievably ours.

Our own driveway.

I parked the car, stood on the grass, turned my face to the blue sky, and spun around and around and around as if I'd never seen a gravel path before. This was it. Line after line, scene after scene, the script was unfolding. The move. The jump. The house. The new beginning. Everything we'd hoped for and dreamed of and prayed about was about to happen.

We were so close to amazing.

~~⁓~~

I was still smiling later that night as I scanned the Internet for comps the bank had requested for the property. I jotted down notes on a few similar plots and started to click out of the website when a listing caught my eye.

It was a farmhouse.

"Self," I scolded. "Don't even think about it. You already have house plans and chicken barn plans, and there's a spinning rooster weather vane with your name on it."

I tried to click away. Really, I did. I tried drinking sweet tea and putting my hair in a messy bun and biting my lip and wrinkling my nose to distract myself. I tried counting the mashed Cheetos on the floor and reminding myself of the script and the green grass between my toes.

But nothing worked.

Softly and sweetly, the house whispered my name. I resisted for a moment longer, summoning my last little bit of strength from the depths of my soul. I clung desperately to my version of the Texas battle cry. "Remember the driveway," I whispered hoarsely as I shook my fist at the sky. "Remember the driveway."

Famous last words.

I opened the listing and let my heart read. It was a three-story white farmhouse with five bedrooms and three bathrooms and ten-foot ceilings and bay windows and a peaked roof with farmhouse molding and a large wooden deck in back. There was a creek and a pond and a barn and acres and acres and acres of land.

And a beauty parlor.

total aside

The term "beauty parlor" may be overstating the glamour a bit. The room was basically a tiny outbuilding on the property with a space where a chair used to be and drawers that were full of old, sticky bobby pins. But I was so giddy about owning it that I was about to enroll in beauty school and see if the cast from Steel Magnolias was available.

I waited for two days before I showed my husband the listing for the farmhouse. How do you begin a conversation like that? How do you explain to someone that a house on the Internet whispered your name without sounding like a candidate for a reality television show? How do you bring up the idea that the building project on the river might be destined to begin and end with a driveway?

My grandmother always said that the way to introduce a man to a random idea is through his stomach.

I took heed.

I spent hours getting ready. I set the table, and I ironed the monogrammed linens, folding them to resemble birds-of-paradise. I cut fresh flowers from the yard, tucking in twigs and lemons to create a centerpiece.

Finally, dinner was ready. With great flourish and fanfare, I arranged everything on an oversized white platter and placed the delicious meal in front of my husband: microwaved Hot Pockets served piping hot, with a side of macaroni and cheese.

His eyes lit up at the sight of all that homemade goodness, and he dug in enthusiastically. We discussed the day for a while and then munched along together in companionable silence. Finally, amid a bite of pepperoni and mozzarella cheese, I broached the subject of the listing.

"Do you remember that episode of *The Love Boat* where Julie the cruise director was going to get married, and the entire staff from the ship traveled all the way to Australia for the wedding?" The words tumbled out in a rush.

Denton stared blankly back at me.

Crickets.

Unfazed, I continued. "Except she didn't. Get married, that is. She was outside the church, standing there in her wedding dress, and Isaac and Gopher were holding her hands, and Captain Stubing was about to give her away, and then the groom never showed up. Remember?" I prodded.

"What? Julie was a cruise director?"

"Exactly!" I nodded approvingly. "You understand. That's exactly what I'm talking about. She was a cruise director who didn't get married, and it all worked out for the best."

He stared helplessly at a piece of pepperoni on his plate as if it held the key to this entire conversation.

"See, that's how I'm feeling about the house we're building on the river. I'm just like Julie, and I don't think I'm going to get married."

A light dawned in his eyes.

Somewhere along the way, my rambling metaphor had clicked.

"You don't want to build?" he said slowly, taking it all in.

"I'm not sure." I bit my lower lip. "I just found this farmhouse listed for sale about ten miles away from here, and it's historic and almost one hundred years old, and there's a pond and a creek and acres and acres, and I know it's not what we agreed on or planned for, and it's not in the script . . ."

My eyes met his across the lemons in the flower arrangement as my words trailed off. "And the house whispered to me," I finished.

He nodded solemnly. He understood. He had been married to me for long enough to comprehend the importance of my discussions with inanimate objects. His brown eyes twinkled as he turned back to his dinner. Then he wiped his mouth with his bird-of-paradise napkin.

"If a house is whispering," he said with a grin, "we should probably pay attention."

⟍ꝑ

Even now I can't believe we flipped the script.

Literally.

I can't believe how everything fell into place, tied up with a bow. I wish things always worked out like that. I wish that changing course in the middle of an existing plan always went according to plan. I wish that every decision I made was the right one and that every day was full of houses that spoke to people.

But life isn't always like that.

The revised scripts we write for our lives aren't always happily-ever-afters. Sometimes we hit our knees and pray until our hearts almost break, but the person we love isn't healed. Sometimes we search endlessly for a job, sending out application after application, but we experience rejection at every turn. We think we've hit bottom—and discover there's even more bottom just a few feet down.

The truth is, we don't have a guarantee that everything will be wrapped up and monogrammed just for us, according to our own plans.

I've had the script pulled out from underneath me more times than I can count. When I discovered I was pregnant with twins, I never planned on having two tiny, two-pound babies. No one told me I'd face brain bleeds and kidney stones and incubators and that fourteen years later, one of the twins would have emergency surgery for a torn retina.

When I got married, I never planned on moving to California.

No way. According to my high school geography teacher, California was on the West Coast, meaning it was more than a thousand miles from home. I couldn't move there. I wanted to live close to my family. I wanted to run around the corner and ask my mother if she was cooking supper.

I never planned for my husband to go off to war. No one mentioned when I said my vows that I'd be facing seven months all by myself after only one year of marriage. I never planned on bombs and an absent husband and giant ships and enemy combatants.

It wasn't in the script.

Not even close.

I'm a planner, a designer. I like to make beauty out of ordinary things and create order out of chaos. But when things like this happen, I'm left with the sobering realization that I'm not the director here. I'm not in charge. "We can make our own plans, but the LORD gives the right answer" (Proverbs 16:1, NLT).

Even though I'm really good at writing Hallmark scripts, there's someone far wiser directing the show.

⁓ꝏ

The day after the Hot Pocket conversation, we called the real estate agent and set up an appointment to look at the house. It was everything the listing said and so much more. There were hardwood floors under the carpets and tall ceilings and farmhouse molding and a tiny door that closed off the staircase to the second floor. There was a butler's pantry and a dining room with columns and two fireplaces and brick on the kitchen wall.

After the tour was over, Denton and I looked at each other as we climbed into the car to leave. Neither of us spoke. We didn't say anything. We didn't have words to express this feeling that was so authentic, so right, and so real. This was it. This was the decision we were supposed to make. This was the home God wanted for us.

We called the agent that night and put in an offer.

"I still can't believe it," I said after the phone call. "I can't believe we changed courses so quickly."

My husband smiled. "It all worked out for the best," he said. "Sometimes change is necessary."

Then he twirled me around, hugged me, and whispered in my ear, "But I'm still not sure that groom should have left Julie at the altar. Couldn't they have rewritten that episode so Julie got married and lived happily ever after?"

He's right, you know.

Everyone knows rewritten scripts always have the best endings.

Flip-the-Script Centerpiece

SUPPLIES

- saw
- 1 piece plywood
  (2 feet by 4 feet or 2 feet by 8 feet)
- 1 piece 120-grit sandpaper
- paintbrush *(optional)*
- 1 quart stain or latex paint
  (optional)

- 5 mason jars
- 7 bunches magnolia leaves
- 5 bunches evergreen branches
- 8–10 long twigs *(nothing fancy—
  from the yard is fine)*
- 5 lemons
- 7 pears

Cut the piece of plywood to 8 inches wide and the length of your table.

 Sand off any rough edges.

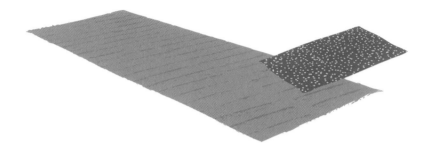

 Stain or paint the plywood to match your decor, and let it dry. Or leave it plain for a more rustic look.

4 Fill the mason jars with magnolia leaves and evergreen branches.

wood stain

5 Add twigs to each of the jars. Your twigs should be 4 to 5 inches taller than the top of the magnolia leaves.

6 Place the jars along the length of the plywood. Scatter the lemons and pears around the base of the jars.

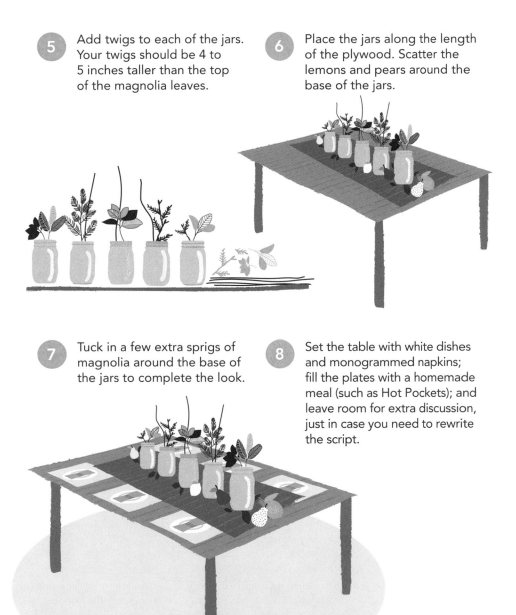

7 Tuck in a few extra sprigs of magnolia around the base of the jars to complete the look.

8 Set the table with white dishes and monogrammed napkins; fill the plates with a homemade meal (such as Hot Pockets); and leave room for extra discussion, just in case you need to rewrite the script.

5

never underestimate a slippery spaghetti ring

LIFE LESSON #5

Regardless of what my second-grade grammar teacher taught me, "Do it yourself" should not be written in second person.

Raise your hand if you've ever watched an entire home make-over take place in under an hour on television.

If you have, you know how the story goes. The host enters the house in the "before" stage, and everyone gasps and averts their eyes and wonders if a mess like that could even be real. The rooms are run down and full of the most pitiful decor you could imagine. The walls are covered with comic book pages that someone once used as wallpaper. The dishwasher is doubling as an herb planter, and abandoned tennis shoes are scattered throughout every room. As the camera follows the host through the house, you shudder and sigh and wonder how the space will ever be livable again.

You leave the room to get popcorn.

After the commercial break, a miracle is taking place! Everything has been ripped out, and the house is just a shell. All the dry-wall and the faux brick fireplace panels and the cabinets and the countertops and the built-ins are gone. Every comic book–covered wall is history.

During the next thirty minutes, as you sit munching on your popcorn, the contractors replace the drywall and add molding and new brick to the fireplace. They install kitchen cabinets and counter-tops in the five minutes it takes you to sip your lemonade. Fifty-five minutes into the show, the homeowners are brought into the newly renovated house. They gasp and immediately start crying, either from joy or relief that the tennis shoes are gone.

All of this in under an hour.

When we left our driveway behind and purchased the farmhouse and started planning our renovation, I was more than ready. I had photos saved to my phone, stacks of notebooks full of ideas, little pictures I'd ripped out of magazines, and an entire Pinterest board devoted to claw-foot bathtubs.

Just like my first perm, I knew this was going to be amazing.

This wasn't my first DIY rodeo. There was the mantel project and the kitchen floor project and the time we tackled an entire bathroom redo. This project was a little different. We'd never completed an entire house renovation before, but how hard could it be? At the risk of stating the obvious, I was kind of a semipro.

I had a BA in decorating shows from cable television.

The day they handed us the keys to the new house, I was so eager to get started on the renovation that I ran over and randomly started pulling down pieces of wallpaper. Between us, there wasn't really a wallpaper-pulling plan. It just sort of happened when I saw the edge of a piece of wallpaper hanging down and decided to peel it off. That peel led to another peel, which led to me standing in the middle of my new dining room with tiny shreds of grape-trellis wallpaper covering my head.

total aside

Wallpaperpulling is fun for only the first ten minutes. Or twenty minutes on a good day, if you have a cute pair of wallpaper-pulling overalls and a matching bandana. Just remember that vinegar and water are your friend, no matter what the infomercials say.

Just like my
first perm, I knew
this was going
to be amazing.

That night I greeted my husband at the door with a messy bun, a rock star T-shirt, black yoga pants covered in firmly attached scraps of grape trellis, and freshly applied red lipstick. I grabbed his hand and dragged him into the dining room to see the progress. Eyes glowing and messy bun dancing, I gestured grandly at the walls.

"Look at what I accomplished today," I said. "Can you even believe it?"

He just stared at the hanging chads of wallpaper. He glanced at the streaks of glue running down the wall and quietly took in the wallpaper scraps that were now sprinkled across the floor like pieces of confetti left over from New Year's Eve. When he finally met my eyes, I heard a noise escape from his mouth. One that sounded suspiciously like a cross between a cough and a laugh.

"Are you laughing?" I frowned.

"Never." He grinned and gently wiped away a stray piece of wallpaper that was stuck to the side of my cheek. "I was just thinking that we need a plan. It will be so much easier if we have a plan and a spreadsheet."

I shot him a quizzical look.

"A plan," I said. "I show you an almost un-wallpapered wall, and you tell me we need a plan? What about just going room by room? Couldn't we start at the front of the house and work backward?" I sighed. "And do we really need a spreadsheet?"

He nodded. "Spreadsheets are a thing," he said. "I'm pretty sure I saw one on that design show you were watching the other day."

At that moment, everything clicked. A lightbulb switched on in my head. He was right. I was pretty sure I'd seen someone on a show with a laptop and a spreadsheet once. That was exactly what we needed for a smooth renovation. That was how we were going to accomplish everything in record time.

A plan.

We jumped headfirst into planning the remodel. We called to get estimates from contractors and plumbers and electricians and carpenters, and by the end of the week, we had a spreadsheet, a budget, and a timeline. It was official. We were ready to renovate.

The first project on the timeline was the combined kitchen and living room. When we started the renovation, the space was two rooms separated by a hallway. The plan was to remove the wall between the rooms to incorporate the hallway into the living room, thereby enlarging the entire space. We also designed a large cutout on the wall between the living room and the kitchen to create the illusion of even more space.

total aside

We ended up installing a transom window in the opening between the two rooms, which was made from a window we found by the side of the road. The moral of the story? What you find on the side of the road is always on clearance.

The first week went according to plan. I felt like I'd stepped directly into a television episode, where the "before" turns into an "after" at lightning speed. Workers descended on our house and removed walls and drywall and ripped up flooring and pulled out cabinets and cut openings between rooms. Everything was moving along so quickly.

At this rate, we'll be done in a month, I thought.

The second week sped by as the wall between the front entry and the living room was opened up, the carpet was ripped out, and the old molding was torn out. Giant piles of debris gathered in our yard, and our driveway was filled with vintage carpet shreds. The kitchen countertops were removed, followed by the cabinets and the stove and the refrigerator and the island. Everything was carried out of the house to be removed later. By the time the teardown was complete, the kitchen had been reduced to a big, empty room with a pipe sticking up in one corner. I couldn't believe the progress.

Then the third week arrived.

And nothing happened.

The weather didn't cooperate. It rained when it should have been sunny. The countertops were on back order. There was a holiday weekend. All the reasons were valid. All the delays were unavoidable. But they were pushing our timeline out further and further.

At first the delay didn't bother me much. The renovation was young, and hope was still springing eternal, and after all, aren't kitchens a little overrated? We adjusted and ate more microwaved dinners and used the bathroom sink to wash our dishes and became close personal friends with the team members at every fast food restaurant in a ten-mile radius.

I laughed in the face of adversity.

But then days turned into weeks, and weeks turned into months as the renovation inched along. We discovered the challenges of renovating a house that has been on this earth for a hundred years. When you tear out a wall, you have a hole in the ceiling; and when you have a hole in the ceiling, you have drywall that needs to be replaced; and when you have drywall that needs to be replaced, you have to tape and bed the drywall, and the tape and bedding mud has to dry before you can paint the ceiling. And so on. It was a giant puzzle.

And we were still missing most of the pieces.

I wish this were the part of the story where I told you that every morning I woke up singing and greeted the birds at my window wearing a blue ball gown and a tiara with dozens of mice ready to help me with my chores. I wish I could tell you that I shrugged off challenges and simply popped another pizza in the microwave. I wish I could say that I smiled and told tomorrow it was only a day away.

Nope.

Not even close.

The longer the renovation took, the more frustrated I became. Frustration gave way to impatience and impatience's second cousin, irritation. We were living in one room and trying to make the most of a difficult situation, but every day the entire situation got worse—along with my attitude. The microwaved foods tasted like cardboard, and the idea of more fast food turned my stomach. Meanwhile, the dirty dishes piled higher in the bathroom sink.

Two months into the renovation, I'd had enough. How much more could one family take? We'd endured two months of washing dishes in the sink. Two months of eating cans of spaghetti rings. Two months of waiting and washing and waiting some more.

This never happens on the television shows.

Ever.

total aside

Never underestimate the gourmet potential of a can of spaghetti rings. Add in a little cheese, fresh herbs, or even a few crackers, and you are one step away from white linen napkins and a four-course meal.

One day the phone rang with some bad news. The sink I wanted wasn't available. It seemed minor, but it wasn't. The sink was the key. It was like a giant game of connecting the thigh bone to the knee bone and then connecting all that to the ankle bone. The floor was waiting on the cabinets, which were waiting on the countertop, which was waiting on the sink . . . *which was nowhere to be found.*

My heart began to race, and I threw down the receiver with all the drama of a soap opera actress who's just learned that her mother's sister's aunt's best friend's brother's cousin was attempting a coup in South Africa.

"ENOUGH!" I screamed at no one in particular. "I've had it. No more."

I stormed into the kitchen to give it a piece of my mind. "No one should have to put up with this," I sputtered. "This was supposed to be fun and creative and the beginning of something wonderful. I want our home. I want it finished. Kitchen, I want you to have a dishwasher and a refrigerator and a sink. Now."

The kitchen just laughed at me.

"Don't you understand? We planned for this," I said. "We had a budget and a design and a timeline . . . and . . . and . . . a spreadsheet!" Tears began to well up in my eyes.

I stood and stared at the kitchen for a few more minutes as the remnants of my temper tantrum faded. Exhausted, I let the emotions dissipate. I turned back toward the hallway to pull out the air mattresses in the back room since the bedrooms still weren't ready. As I opened the bathroom door to pull out the sheets, I saw it.

A giant stack of dirty dishes in the bathroom sink.

Layer upon layer of plates and cups and bowls, covered with a film of day-old spaghetti sauce. I stared in disbelief. No one had done the dishes? Now it was my job to handle the renovation and clean up around the house *and* do the dishes? As if to mock me, one lone spaghetti ring slid off a plate and into the dirty water.

I rolled my eyes with self-righteous indignation and marched toward the dishes with the fire of battle in my eyes. This was it. I'd take care of this situation. I was going to wash those dishes like they'd never been washed before. I ran the water, poured in the soap, and started picking out spaghetti rings one by one and flinging them toward the trash can.

I reached for the plate at the very top of the layer of dishes.

Then, as if in slow motion, the stack toppled slightly, righted itself for a moment, and with one final wobble, came crashing down to the floor. I tried frantically to grab the pile of dishes, and somehow, I caught a bowl with one hand and a plate with the other. I was reaching out to hook a mug with my pinkie when I felt my right foot slide on something. With my hands waving and my arms winding around in circles, I gasped as my legs buckled underneath me. I landed face-first amid the chaos of the bathroom floor.

The culprit responsible for my fall? A spaghetti ring.

When I was brave enough to open my eyes, I saw a scene of horror surrounding me. Shards of bowls and cups and plates littered the bathroom floor. It looked like a minitornado had spun through the room, leaving spaghetti water in its wake. I closed my eyes again and started to sob.

"Why, Lord?" I wailed. "Why is this taking so long? Why did you even bring us to this place? Why did you lead us here? Why did you choose this house for us if it's never ever going to be finished?"

The sobs subsided, and I lay for what seemed like hours on the floor. Eventually I raised myself to my knees and winced as a piece of a dinner plate dented my elbow. I looked at the dishes and the mess, and in that moment, I wanted to gather up my family and my pride and walk out the front door. Never to return again.

I leaned over to pick up a bowl with a crack on one side. I studied it for a moment, wondering if I should keep it as a souvenir of the day I met the bathroom floor for the first time. I turned it over in my hands, looking at it with new eyes. This bowl had been created by a master potter. The lines of the piece were beautifully and wonderfully made. Every detail, every line of the dish had been crafted with skill and purpose. And the crack? Instead of detracting from the beauty, it merely enhanced the design.

"Just like me," I whispered. "I'm a cracked pot. I'm full of flaws and imperfections and weaknesses. But I, too, was designed by a master craftsman. And I, too, am beautifully and wonderfully made."

Suddenly, without warning, peace flooded my soul. I knew without a doubt that the Creator had plans for me. Just like it was written: "You, LORD, are our Father. We are the clay, you are the potter; we are all the work of your hand" (Isaiah 64:8).

This journey to our new home was no mistake. Moving to the country and buying a farmhouse and changing the script and sweating through these renovations—all of it—was as it was supposed to be. An amazing, gifted Potter had laid out his plans for my life from my very first breath. And he knew. He knew the timeline for the house. He knew every detail of the timeline and the location of every piece of drywall and every entry on the spreadsheet.

I laid the bowl on the counter and reached for the broom and started sweeping up the tiny pieces of cups and spaghetti-covered plates. I stopped midsweep and smiled to myself. *Not only does he have a plan for my life, he understands room layouts and curtains and drapes and antique floors and bathroom sinks.*

Of course he does.

He's the master designer.

Pieces-of-a-House Wall Art

+ safety glasses
+ dust mask
+ 1 piece 60-grit sandpaper
+ 1 piece plywood *(½ inch thick, 16 inches by 16 inches)*
+ hammer
+ nails *(1¼ inch long)*
+ 4 pieces pine *(1 inch by 1 inch by 16 inches)*
+ pencil
+ 1 piece graphite paper
+ rough outline of your house *(You can use a photo-editing program to transform a picture into a sketch.)*
+ safety gloves

+ assorted pieces broken pottery *(purchased in a package from a craft store)*
+ 1 bottle tile adhesive
+ 1 tub tile grout
+ wet rag
+ damp sponge

1. Before starting the project, put on the safety glasses and the dust mask.

2. Sand the plywood to provide a rough surface for the pottery pieces to adhere to.

3 Nail two pieces of 16-inch-long pine to the top and bottom of the front side of the plywood. Cut the other two pieces of 16-inch-long pine to fit the gap and nail them to the sides of the plywood. This will be the frame for your artwork.

4 Transfer the rough outline of your house onto the plywood using a pencil and the graphite paper.

5 Wearing safety gloves, lay out the pieces of pottery on the house design. Group colors together to create layers of the house. For example, use darker pieces for the roof, lighter pieces for the sides of the house, and shiny pieces for the windows. Note that the pieces don't have to fit together perfectly.

6 After all the pieces have been laid out, glue them in place with tile adhesive. Let the adhesive dry for twenty-four hours.

Take a scoop of tile grout and push the grout between the pieces of pottery. Be sure to get as much grout as you can between the pieces.

 Remove the excess grout with a wet rag. Let it dry slightly.

tile grout

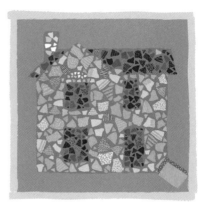

9 Wipe the film from the grout off the pieces of pottery with a damp sponge. Repeat until all the pieces are clean.

10 Add the artwork to your bookcase as a reminder that even the most broken pieces can come together to create something beautiful.

CRAFTS

CERAMICS

6

a floor without end

LIFE LESSON #6

*Floors are a lot like people. Just
when you think you've discovered all
there is, another layer shows up.*

Confession time: I'm not that into kitchens. I know most people love them. I wish I did, but they are full of activities I don't understand, like broiling and blanching and roasting and rendering and braising and reconstituting. Kitchens have drawers full of foreign gizmos and gadgets, like mandolines and juicers and sifters and shakers and colanders and spiralizers. To me, kitchens are mysterious places where flour turns into biscuits and cucumbers reintroduce themselves as pickles and a lowly avocado is transformed into a little slice of heaven.

By someone other than me.

Simply put, I'm just not fluent in dough or mashed-up fruit.

There was a time when I thought I could cook. Once, when my husband was just my boyfriend, I offered to make him lunch. We were both home from college for the summer, and I thought our relationship had progressed to the point where cooking should make an appearance.

This was a really big step for me.

I twisted my add-a-bead necklace for luck, called his house on a phone with a cord, and invited him over to my parents' house for lunch. I explained that I wanted to treat him by making him anything he wanted and assured him the world could be his oyster.

Literally.

I got out a pen and paper and waited for his answer with bated breath.

"Pancakes," he replied without skipping a beat.

On my end of the phone, I rolled my powder-blue eyelids. *Really? Pancakes?*

"Pancakes are great," I said patiently. "But you don't need to keep it simple. I've got this. I can make anything. What about filet mignon or braised pork chops or even grilled chicken stuffed with ricotta cheese?"

"Don't worry about it," he said. "Those all sound great, but I think I just want regular, plain, ordinary pancakes."

Sigh.

Regular, plain, ordinary pancakes coming right up.

Now I'd never made pancakes before. Truthfully, I'd never really made anything except chocolate chip cookies. I'd never heard of Bisquick or other mixes, and the only pancakes I knew about were the ones that showed up on my plate at a restaurant along with some crispy bacon.

It's pancakes, I thought. *How hard can it be? After all, I know how to read a recipe.*

I started by putting milk and sugar and eggs in the mixing bowl. Next I added baking powder and salt and butter and flour and whisked according to the directions. Then I stopped midwhisk and stared at the bowl.

What is this? I thought.

The batter in that bowl didn't look anything like chocolate chip cookie dough. Not even close. It was a hot mess. There were bubbles covering the entire surface and bits of flour everywhere. And the worst part? The dough was runny. I watched in awe as rivers of runny dough slopped around, completely covering the inside of the bowl.

Seriously?

I panicked. Something was wrong. *Very* wrong. How was I going to form the dough into balls to press into the pan to make pancakes if the dough was runny? I frantically scanned the recipe again. *Milk? Check. Eggs? Check. Flour? Check.*

Wait a minute.

Ahh, flour! That's what I needed. *Extra flour will make the batter so much easier to work with,* I thought.

So, I added more flour to the bowl and stirred it in. It still wasn't enough.

Just one more cup, I thought. *It's almost there.* But I had the sense it just needed a little something extra. I opened the freezer and had a light-bulb moment. Why not add frozen blueberries? Now I was set. I was ready to create the most amazing pancakes the world had ever tasted.

To this day, I'm not sure what made me think to add those blueberries. I just found myself reaching into the freezer, pulling out a bag, and kneading the berries into the batter until it turned blue. I think the skillet made me do it.

I glanced at the clock, realized I was running out of time, and decided to press the entire blue ball of dough into the frying pan to make one large pancake. In my rush, I accidentally burned the pancake on both sides.

No worries, I thought as I added powdered sugar to cover the burn marks, topped it off with frozen blueberry garnish, and rushed lunch to the table just as the doorbell rang. I opened the door and escorted my future husband to the table.

Oh, the meal that was waiting for him!

His eyes lit up when he saw the giant powdered-sugared delicacy

I had set on the table. He put his napkin in his lap, reached for his fork in anticipation, and dug into his lunch. Without warning, rivers of blue goo spilled onto his plate from the epicenter of that undercooked, yet oddly overcooked blueberry pancake.

My eyes widened, and I tried desperately not to burst into tears.

He glanced at me, took a deep breath, and scooped up the chunks of blue goo and powdered sugar. Without flinching, he shoved a forkful of pancake into his mouth between gritted teeth and chewed it manfully. I couldn't help but notice the painful grin on his face, as if he were a contestant on *Survivor* trying to win blankets and fire-starting equipment.

He swallowed, guzzled a gulp of orange juice, put down his fork, and never took another bite. Instead, he distracted me with his twinkly brown eyes and funny stories about work as we ignored the blue goo oozing onto the plate between us.

Somehow, despite smashed blueberries and burned flapjacks, our relationship managed to survive. Denton married me a little over a year later, knowing all about my cooking skills.

Or lack thereof.

As for that pancake? It sealed my cooking fate. I never really wanted to experiment in the kitchen again. I mean, I tried to cook. *Truly.* But recipes and kitchens intimidated me.

Especially kitchens that took three months to renovate.

⌒ᗡ

At the risk of stating the obvious, home renovation is not for the faint of heart. There were days when I felt like a mountain climber. There were days when I wondered if our marriage would survive. It was like I was a teenager again, fighting with my raging DIY hormones.

Conversations in our house sounded a lot like this:

Me: Sweetie, I just found the cutest tile for the bathroom. I saw it on HGTV, and I googled it. It's cement and looks like it came from an abandoned chateau in France.

Denton (in the middle of installing floor molding): Hmm. Cement tile?

Me: Oh good. So you like it too? It's just a little more expensive than the white subway tile from Home Depot.

Denton (arching his eyebrows): How much more expensive?

Me (shrugging nonchalantly and not meeting his eyes): Not too much more. About twenty-five dollars a square foot.

Denton (putting down the molding and giving me his full attention): What? Twenty-five dollars a square foot? The other tile was only a few dollars per square foot. That's not in the budget.

Me (smiling encouragingly): We can make it work. I can give up something else. Maybe the tub? Tubs are overrated.

Denton (rolling his eyes): I don't see cement tile in the bathroom's future.

Me (stomping my cute, flip-flopped foot): I don't feel like you understand me or my vision.

Denton (turning back to finish the molding): I love your vision. I just wish it was better friends with our budget.

And on and on and on it went.

The push and pull between us. The late-night disagreements. The hours spent remodeling in vain because the project ended up needing a do-over. The ever-present budget. All the learning curves that never really got learned.

The struggle was real.

We were two months into the renovation when we decided to tackle the floor. We had already removed the walls and the countertops and the cabinets. All the wallpaper had been scraped off, and we'd taken out the appliances and started framing the shelving in the butler's pantry. It was time for an easy project.

Famous last words.

One day my husband told me he was starting on the floor, and I told him I was heading to Walmart.

"It shouldn't take long," he said. "It's just laminate. I'm going to pull up the planks so we can see if we need to make any repairs on the original floors underneath."

Four hours later, I returned with a microwave pizza, a new pair of yoga pants, and a set of Adirondack chairs. I walked into the kitchen and almost stumbled over my husband, who was lying on the floor with a flashlight.

"What are you looking at?" I asked, dropping the bags in the hallway.

He didn't say anything. He just pointed at the half-removed floor.

I peered between the floorboards and saw a hint of pattern and woven fibers.

"Seriously?" I groaned. "Is that carpet?"

"I can't believe it," he said. "I pulled up the laminate, and instead of hardwood floors, there's a layer of old carpeting underneath."

"I'm sorry," I said. "I know it seems a little overwhelming, but don't worry, you've got this." I headed to the microwave. "The rest of the laminate should come right up, and then you can pull up the carpet and we can look at the original floors."

I popped the pizza in the microwave and tried on my new yoga pants for him, and then we sat in the Adirondack chairs under the stars and discussed why anyone would have old carpet in a kitchen. We laughed and assured each other that tomorrow was another day. Tomorrow was the day we would see our floor.

Except.

Except when he pulled up the laminate flooring and removed the old carpeting, he wasn't done. Not even close. There was another layer of linoleum under the carpet and another layer of vintage carpeting under that. Four layers of flooring. One layer on top of another layer on top of another.

I guess floor removal wasn't a thing in 1918.

Finally, after the fourth layer, our floor showed up. One day I walked into the house to see my husband standing on the original floor in the middle of the kitchen. He looked like a warrior just returning home from a battle in foreign lands, with bits of vanquished carpet and linoleum stacked under his feet. He was a conquering hero.

I wanted to hug him.

I wanted to celebrate.

I wanted to take my scarf from my medieval pointed hat and drape it around the neck of my champion.

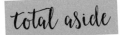

I'm pretty sure the inhabitants of little houses on the prairie never put down carpet in their kitchens. They were much more selective with their flooring choices. Which is why I'm sure it was a much easier time to live. Well played, Laura Ingalls.

Just as I was getting ready to soar across the room into his arms, I noticed the sunlight glinting off something on the kitchen floor. I blinked twice and looked again. It was a nail sticking up from the floor. Then I noticed another nail. And another. And another. There were nails everywhere—hundreds of them spread out across the floor.

"What in the world?" I asked, pointing to the hardware aisle currently doubling as my kitchen floor. "Where did all those nails come from?"

"That's how they attached the last layer of flooring," Denton said. "I went to pull it up, and it was so old that it just disintegrated and left the nails behind." He took a breath. "Don't worry. It's no big deal. I'm going to pull them up."

And he tried.

I stood in the hallway for hours and listened as grunts and

guttural howls and sounds that reminded me of a horror movie I saw in high school poured out of the kitchen. I watched as he pulled and twisted and turned and tugged with all his might. I smiled encouragingly as he slammed the door and left to get a crowbar from the hardware store.

All to no avail.

It was an impossible task. It made the War of 1812 look like a schoolroom brawl. It was an epic tale of man versus nails. Those nails had been in the floor for almost a hundred years, and they were winning.

Hours later I tiptoed around the nails into the kitchen. There was my husband, leaning against the wall with his head resting on his hands. His shirt was soaked with sweat, and he was surrounded by twisted nails that were still stuck in the antique floor.

He looked so defeated. My heart broke as he stood there, dejected, in the midst of a victorious army of hardware.

I made my way over to him.

"You've got this," I whispered. "It's just a floor. These are just nails. They can't keep winning forever."

His only response was to shrug his shoulders and kick at a bent nail with his foot.

"Don't worry," I said. "I know a guy who knows a guy who has a friend who might be a nail puller. We can call him tomorrow, and I know they could knock this out in a day."

He put down the hammer and pulled me against his chest. I could feel his heart beating double time against my cheek.

"I feel like such a failure," he said. "We shouldn't have to call anyone. I should be able to pull up nails. I'm in charge here. I should

You are my hero.
You've shown me
this journey
through God's eyes.

be able to handle it." He paused. "I feel like I let you down," he whispered.

"You?" I said, startled. "You, let me down? Are you kidding?"

I pulled away from him and stared into his eyes. "You are my hero. You've shown me this journey through God's eyes, and you provide for our family, and you drove me across the country, and you were my rock when I had a showdown with spaghetti rings. You didn't blink when I told you I wanted to buy this farmhouse, and you've spent every night building and framing and pulling and prodding and taking on an army of steadfast nails."

He stared at me. "Do you mean that? I haven't disappointed you?"

"Never," I assured him. "I couldn't have taken a single step without you."

He smiled as if a weight had been lifted from his shoulders. His eyes danced in the dim light of the kitchen. Then he laughed and hugged me again.

"I'll call the guys tomorrow. I promise." My voice was muffled as I snuggled into his arms. "And those nails? They're history. After the guys pull them out, we can work on getting the floor finished and the renovation back on track. Things are looking up around here."

Then a thought struck me, and I laughed. "Besides, you've already tasted my pancakes. It had to be all downhill from there."

You-Nailed-It Floorcloth

+ 1 piece standard linoleum
  (6 feet by 9 feet)
+ scissors
+ paintbrush
+ 1 quart latex primer
+ yardstick
+ pencil

+ 1 roll painter's tape
+ 4 bottles light gray acrylic paint
+ 4 bottles dark gray acrylic paint
+ 3 bottles black acrylic paint
+ 1 quart water-based
  polyurethane

Flip over the piece of linoleum. (Since this project is done on the reverse side of the linoleum, be sure to select linoleum with a simple pattern on the front to prevent any of the pattern from pressing through to the back.) Use the scissors to trim off any stray pieces on the edges of the linoleum.

Paint the linoleum with the primer. Let it dry completely.

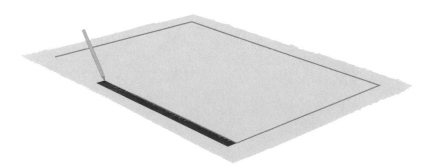

Sketch out your floorcloth design on the linoleum. I've designed a basic pattern to get you started, but feel free to make this project your own and create your own design.

Using a yardstick and a pencil, draw a 10-inch wide border around the edge of the linoleum. Draw a 2-inch border inside the 10-inch border. The inner rectangle should now be 4 feet by 7 feet.

5 Place the painter's tape along the inside edge of the first pencil line (so all ten inches will be painted). Place more painter's tape along the outside edge of the second pencil line (so the full 4-foot by 7-foot rectangle will be painted).

6 Press down all the edges of the tape, and then flatten the tape with the edge of a credit card or a library card to ensure that the tape is completely adhered to the surface.

7 Paint the center rectangle with the light gray paint.

8 Paint the 10-inch border with the dark gray paint. Remove all the tape, and then let the floorcloth dry completely, about twenty-four hours.

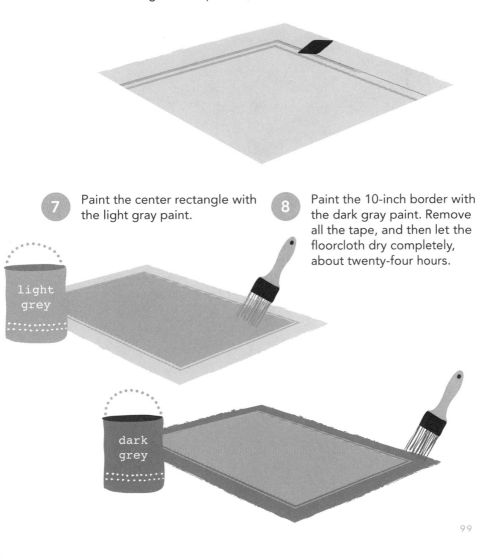

light grey

dark grey

9

After the paint is dry, tape off the outer sides of the 2-inch border with painter's tape.

Paint the 2-inch border with black paint. Remove the tape, and then let the floorcloth dry completely, about twenty-four hours.

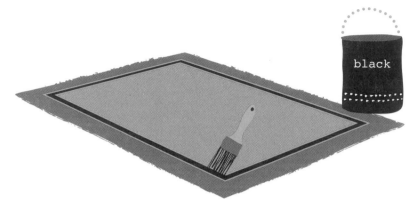

black

11 In the light gray center, draw a checkerboard pattern using a yardstick and a pencil. Mark off four 12-inch-by-12-inch squares across and seven 12-inch-by-12-inch squares down.

12 Tape around every other square outside the pencil lines. Paint the inside of the taped-off squares with dark gray paint. Remove the tape and let the floorcloth dry completely, about twenty-four hours.

13 If you want to personalize the floorcloth with a monogram or quote or any other design, do it now, before you seal the floorcloth.

14 Seal the floorcloth with two coats of water-based polyurethane. Let it dry between coats, and then let it dry completely before using it.

15 Place the floorcloth on your floor as a reminder that the key to surviving the challenges of a home remodel is encouragement.

7

trash-talking

LIFE LESSON #7

The only really smart thing to do with trash is to give it another chance. It's never a good idea to keep a good piece of garbage down.

Have you ever heard a three-county cry before?

You know . . . a cry that erupts from the very epicenter of your soul and wrenches your guts and your heart with it? A cry that bubbles beneath the surface, churning and twisting and turning, just bursting at the seams to come out? You try in vain to contain it by pressing your stomach and staring at the ceiling and crossing your legs and reciting the multiplication tables backward, but just when you least expect it, it works its way up, hovers on the tip of your tongue, and releases a noise into the universe that sounds like a cross between the howl of a hyena and the jubilant yell of a lumberjack watching the last tree fall.

That cry.

The cry I uttered the day the renovation was finished. After eight months, we were done. I couldn't believe it. There was an open concept family room and a living room where there used to be a hallway. The kitchen now had nail-free, heart pine wood floors that had been sanded and stained and polished to a brilliant shine, reflecting the sparkling light of the new chandeliers. The contractors added farmhouse built-ins in the butler's pantry, a new sink in the bathroom, new molding, and transom windows in the family room. Fifteen rooms had been stripped of wallpaper and were now painted in soft, welcoming khakis and grays. The house was fresh and clean and smelled like new.

Except.

Except that most of the house was furniture-less. It was trying to look like it was furnished. *Truly.* There was a random pair of dining room chairs around a white plastic table trying to pass themselves off as a dining room set. In the family room, there were two bedraggled wingback chairs (with more back than wing) hanging their heads in shame. In an effort to downsize, we'd sold most of our furniture before we left Texas, and our new house was feeling a little lost without it.

And the worst part? We were almost flat broke. Most of our furniture money had been eaten up with the remodel, and there just wasn't anything left.

Undaunted, I took our lack of funds as a challenge. *Furniture? That's all we needed?* Wasn't I a champion do-it-yourselfer? Hadn't I cut my teeth on HGTV? Hadn't I devoted the greater part of my existence to embracing shows where designers were given paper plates and soda cans and seventy-five dollars to furnish an entire room?

At the risk of stating the obvious, I was made for a situation like this.

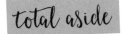

I once watched a show where a designer created an entire piece of wall art from leftover water bottles she'd found by the curb. It was amazing and terrifying all at the same time. Maybe this is a good time to remind ourselves that just because you can doesn't mean you should.

I started furnishing the house at the place all good makeovers begin: the thrift store. I found a bookcase they almost paid me to take away and flipped it upside down to make a hutch. I took a side table with a damaged top, glued cork to the surface, and turned it into a message center. In the corner of another store, I discovered a box of mismatched dishes and covered the walls with them. I found a giant pallet at the feed store and added hinges attached to a fold-down top to transform it into a desk. I hung it vertically on the wall and told myself that thrifting was so much better than sliced bread.

Especially if you are not a baker.

Next I shopped yard sales. I found a few dresser drawers that I transformed into organizers by adding wheels, and I found a table with a finish that looked like the Pilgrims had carried it with them through the stormy seas on the *Mayflower*. I bought baskets that I spray-painted with numbers on the front. Then I placed the baskets along the top shelves of the butler's pantry and filled them with extra linens to keep myself organized. I found a table with a damaged top, bought a four-dollar package of wood shims from the home improvement store, and glued them in a herringbone pattern on the top. I did cartwheels in the parking lot when I found a dining room table for ten dollars and an ottoman for seven dollars and a set of wooden chairs for two dollars each.

It was like winning the furniture lottery, except so much better. I painted and stained and distressed, and by the time I was finished, the house had rooms full of furniture. I was almost there. All that remained was artwork for the walls, and I was done. So I braced myself, squared my shoulders, and headed where few dare to venture—the one remaining uncharted frontier.

The trash.

Bright and early every Monday on trash day, I'd sit behind the wheel of an old, battered pickup truck wearing an outfit that can only be described as so close to amazing. Usually it was yoga pants decorated with the perfect combination of holes and paint, a rock star T-shirt with grease stains from a long-ago taco dinner, and a glittery hair clip.

I wore the T-shirt and yoga pants in case I got dirty. I wore the hair clip just to keep it classy. Driving those winding country roads at a snail's pace, I stalked the trash like a cougar stalks its prey. The thrill of the hunt and coffee kept me going back Monday after Monday. You wouldn't believe the trash I found. One morning I discovered a four-poster bed, and the next week I found a wingback chair. I brought home architectural pieces and spools and drawers and frames and baskets and iron fragments.

Once I found a table that was broken in half, and my yoga pants and I rejoiced. I took the two broken pieces, attached them to the wall, and created bedside tables. Nothing was off limits. Nothing was sacred. There wasn't a piece I found that couldn't be fixed with a little glue and a power washer.

I was the trash whisperer.

total aside

If you are a trash hunter, just remember that the power washer is your friend. I once brought home some old wood, made a sign out of it, and hung it on the wall. A week later I found a pile of sawdust. As it turned out, the wood had bugs. A power washer could have prevented the entire infestation. I'm all for inviting people over, but I draw the line at unwanted guests.

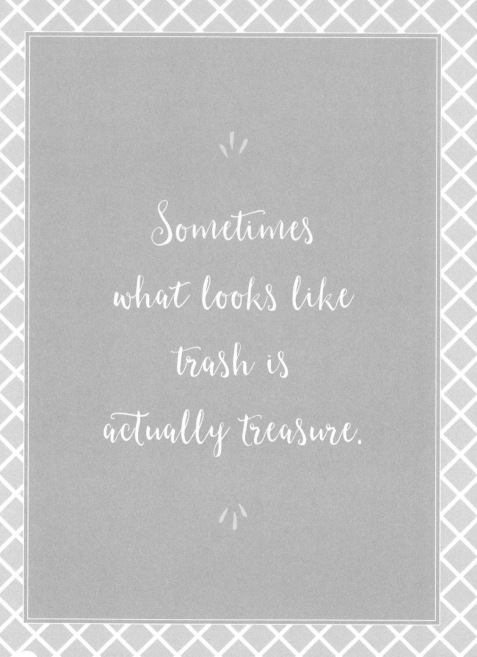

Sometimes
what looks like
trash is
actually treasure.

Slowly but surely, home decor that had once been disguised as junk filled the rooms of our home. Room by room, penny by penny, dime by dime, I decorated the house. I reupholstered a chair with a sheet and moved it into the family room, along with wooden chairs with schoolhouse backs. At last, everything was coming together. Our house was finally becoming a home.

But one thing eluded me. There was one decorating dilemma I just couldn't seem to solve. Try as I might, I couldn't figure out what to do with the giant blank wall in the living room. I hung up a gallery wall, but it looked a little flat. I tried filling the wall with two giant arrows, but it looked like I was lost. I switched and rearranged and moved and tweaked, but every time I arrived at the same conclusion.

I had absolutely, positively, no idea what to do.

Then one day I was minding my own trash-whispering business, driving to the convenience store to buy gas-station pizza for dinner. Driving behind an oversized piece of farm equipment at the overwhelming speed of 7.75 miles per hour, with my messy bun dancing along to the awe-inspiring lyrics of "Eye of the Tiger," I noticed the sun glinting off something by the side of the road.

Intrigued, I turned the car around and headed back for a second look. It was a window, but it didn't look like any window I'd ever seen before. It was the Goliath of windows. It was giant and oversized, approximately seven feet wide and five feet tall, and it had row upon row of windowpanes with chipped white trim. Slowly I counted the panes.

"One, two, three, four, five," I whispered to myself in anticipation. "Times one, two, three, four . . ."

I had to pause. I almost couldn't breathe from the excitement. I had already counted twenty panes, and I still wasn't done.

"Five, six, seven, eight," I finished.

My words trailed off and bounced along the driveway as I stared in awe at the window. Forty panes. Forty wonderful, incredible panes. And the most amazing part? They were all in one window. In my long and storied history of thrifting and yard saling and estate-sale shopping, this was the finest piece of architectural salvage I'd ever discovered. This was my solution to the blank-wall-decorating dilemma—I was sure of it. These forty panes could become something so much more than a window.

It could be a calendar.

Face to face, out in the heat
Hangin' tough, stayin' hungry

The words to the song boomed from the speakers in the car. Survivor was right. This was my moment. I had seen the eye of the tiger. I had tasted the thrill of the fight. With everything that was with me, I was rising up to the challenge of my rivals.

This was my destiny.

A good rock anthem has gotten me through many a rough patch. Never underestimate the power of eyeing the tiger, celebrating good times, or fighting for your right to party.

Waving good-bye to the window with a promise of a future relationship, I hopped back in the car and drove home as quickly as I could. I parked in front and ran up the driveway in search of my husband. I found him trimming bushes and watering the lawn in the backyard.

"You have to come with me!" I grabbed his hand. "We have to go now. We have to get it before someone else does."

To his credit, he never paused. He never asked why. He never even asked what "it" was. He simply put down the trimmers, turned off the water, grabbed his keys, and calmly headed toward the car.

"Not the car," I said impatiently. "We need the truck. It's not going to fit in the car. Wait until you see it! It's . . . well, it's so BIG."

On the way to get the window, I told him everything. Amid hand waving and gasps and exclamations, I explained about Survivor and the winding road and the snail's pace of the farm equipment. Then I paused for emphasis and launched into a detailed description of the window: that incredible, wonderful, amazing piece of architectural salvage that had called my name.

"A window?" He raised an eyebrow. "That's what all this fuss is about? Are you sure we really need another window? We have dozens of them just sitting around the workshop."

"You don't understand," I said. "Those windows can't even compare."

I paused, and with a nervous glance back at the truck bed, I added, "I sure hope it fits in the back of the truck."

Five minutes later, we pulled up beside the window. There it sat in all its glory, the sun glinting off each of its forty panes. My husband got out of the truck and stood silently, assessing the situation.

"Well," I prodded. "What do you think?"

He circled the window once with methodical precision. Then he turned and circled back again, his hand rubbing the stubble on his chin.

"You were right," he said slowly. "That is some window."

To this day, I'm still not sure how the two of us managed to get the window in the back of the truck. We each grabbed an end, staggered backward, and wobbled this way and that. Finally, we managed to get a corner in. Then we lifted the side around and tried to wedge it against the back of the truck to support the panes.

Except.

Except it didn't exactly fit. It was so close. It was almost there. We maneuvered the window this way and that until at last only about a quarter of the window hung over the edge. About eight panes defiantly stuck their necks out of the truck bed, as if to say, "You might have picked us up, but you'll never tame us."

I hopped into the cab of the truck and waited for my husband to secure the window. Then we were off, jostling down winding country roads with our precious cargo. I was overwhelmed with joy, barely able to believe we'd secured such a treasure. Then, in the midst of my excitement, I saw something I'll never forget.

A neighbor cheering us on.

He walked out onto his porch and waved at us as we drove by. I couldn't believe it. I waved back, pointed to the window, and lifted my arms in a victory cheer. He laughed and clapped his hands, and I couldn't help but wonder if this was the first time a rescued window had received a standing ovation.

And that neighbor wasn't the only one.

An entire group of people stood on the front porch at the next house, awaiting our arrival. Four houses down the road we were met with more celebration. More waves. I watched in awe as we drove by house after house, porch after porch—all full of people cheering our window down the road.

My heart overflowed.

Those cheering fans understood. They got it. This broken, worn-out, chipped window that had been discarded and cast aside had a value beyond compare. It wasn't trash. It wasn't junk. It was full of beauty and purpose and charm, with a story written in every line of its forty panes.

I knew all about feeling discarded. I knew what it was like to be picked last for the team. I knew what it was like to try out for the play and be assigned a character part because I wasn't "leading lady" material. I knew what it was like to go to a conference and stand alone in the middle of a reception with no one to talk to. I knew what it was like to have someone whisper when you wore hand-me-downs.

I identified with that window more than I wanted to admit.

And suddenly, in that moment, the window's story became my own. I, too, was broken. I, too, was chipped. I, too, knew what it was like to feel abandoned and unwanted. On my best of days, I was imperfect and flawed and mismatched and a little crooked and off kilter.

Until I was rescued.

Until I was saved.

Until a perfect Savior reached down, plucked me from the side of the road, wrapped me in his embrace, and washed me clean.

I once was lost, but now I'm found,
Was blind, but now I see.

We removed the panes and cut a giant piece of plywood to fit behind the window frame. Then I painted the plywood with chalkboard paint and made labels for the days of the week for each of the columns. Then I primed the chalkboard, added a burlap sack of chalk, and sure enough, it was exactly what the big wall in the living room needed. But even better than solving my home decorating dilemma, I discovered a few things that day. I learned that decorating a house on a budget comes with some obstacles. I learned that good neighbors are priceless. I learned the importance of changing into a cute outfit if I plan on driving a window down the road. But most important?

I learned that sometimes what looks like trash is actually treasure. And that God doesn't ever make junk.

Calendar Worthy of a Parade

- saw
- 1 piece plywood
  (½ inch thick, 4 feet by 8 feet)
- 120-grit sandpaper
- paintbrush
- 1 quart white latex primer
- 1 quart chalkboard paint
- 2 pieces pine
  (1 inch by 2 inches by 60 inches)
- 2 pieces pine
  (1 inch by 2 inches by 37 inches)
- 3 pieces pine
  (1 inch by 1 inch by 58 inches)

- 6 pieces pine
  (1 inch by 1 inch by 34 inches)
- 1 quart white latex paint
- hammer
- nails (1¼ inches)
- 7 wood blocks
  (1 inch by 2 inches by 3 inches)
- pencil
- 1 piece graphite paper (optional)
- 1 bottle black acrylic paint
- wood glue
- chalk
- eraser

Cut the plywood board to 60 inches by 39 inches. Sand the plywood to remove any rough edges.

2 Paint one entire side of the piece of plywood with the primer and let it dry.

3 Paint the same side of the plywood with chalkboard paint and let it dry. Paint a second coat and let it dry.

4 Paint each of the pine boards with primer. When they're dry, paint each of the pine boards with white paint. Let them dry.

5 To form the frame nail the pieces of pine to the large piece of plywood. Lay one 60-inch-long piece of pine flush to the top of the plywood so that the 2-inch side faces forward. Nail it in place. Nail the second 60-inch piece of pine to the bottom. Trim the 37-inch pieces of pine to fit the gap and nail them to each side.

6 Now that the outer frame is complete, it's time to nail boards to the center to create the days of the week. Trim the three 58-inch pieces of pine to fit the gap and nail them horizontally across the center of the frame, equally spaced. This should create four rows.

7 Next, create rectangles for the days of the week with the 34-inch pieces of pine. Cut them to fit the gaps, and arrange them evenly across the four rows, six per row, to create seven rectangles per row. Nail them in place.

8 Paint the seven small wood blocks with primer and let them dry. Then paint them with white paint and let them dry. Paint each of the days of the week onto the blocks with black acrylic paint. You can freehand the days of the week or print them out on your printer, transfer them to the wood with graphite paper, and then paint the traced lines.

9 Using wood glue, attach these blocks over the correct columns of days.

 10 Allow the calendar to dry overnight, then sand the calendar frame lightly with 120-grit sandpaper to distress.

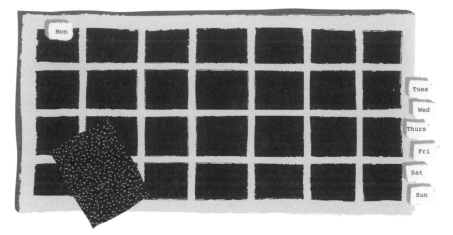

11 Prepare the chalkboard for use by covering each of the rectangles with chalk. Erase. Your oversized calendar is ready for whatever the month holds!

12 Add family activities or events to the days of the week. As you do, let the chalkboard serve as a reminder to always look beneath the surface to see the potential that's always there.

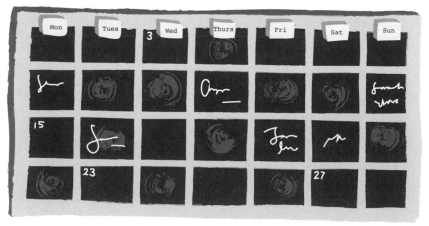

8

the roast that went
to garden club

LIFE LESSON #8

Never judge a person until you've

walked a mile in their yoga pants

or cooked a roast in their kitchen.

I grew up with "the wave."

Southerners are known for it. If you've ever driven down a winding country road somewhere south of the Mason-Dixon Line, you've met the wave. Every car, every tractor, every combine, every truck with its bumper taped up with duct tape on one side is well versed in the wave. Sometimes you don't know the driver. Sometimes the person might be your cousin's sister-in-law's best friend's brother's aunt's new boyfriend. And sometimes you don't recognize the person at all. It doesn't matter.

You still wave back.

The wave was one of the things I was most looking forward to with our move. When you live in the city, customs like that get kind of lost. Everyone is so busy with their day planners and yoga and coffee and meetings and lunches and meet-ups and events that somewhere along the way they forget all about the wave. And being part of a one-sided wave?

Super awkward.

From the moment we jumped, I was excited about life in the country and everything that came with it. I was ready for waves and square dances and barn raisings and potlucks and neighbors who dropped off pies and sweet tea on the porch and gender-reveal parties for farm animals.

I quickly discovered, however, that social life in the country would take some adjusting to. Don't get me wrong—everyone was nice. Everyone was friendly. People said hello and smiled at me in aisle seven of the dollar store. And yes, everyone waved.

But I wanted more. I wanted to meet people and make friends and learn about this new place. I wanted to go to lunch at the neighbor's

Through my
vulnerability,
I had opened an
unexpected door
for friendship.

house and discover new ways of doing things and go out to dinner with friends. But instead? I just sat at my house and waited for the phone to ring.

It never did.

Then one day I got tired of waiting. I pulled myself up by my yoga pants and gave myself a lecture about reaching out instead of moping around waiting to be asked to join the party. So I signed up for the canning club and a sewing class and the homemaker's association committee and a shoe drive and the mothers-of-baseball-players group.

It was exhausting.

total aside

One really rough day my husband asked me why I was talking about planting corn. I grimaced and muttered something to myself about being a Roman. He told me not to worry. He was pretty sure Romans grew grapes instead.

Everything was so new, and the learning curve was so steep, and I wasn't sure any of it was for me. I tried. I really did. I spent hours canning tomatoes when all I really wanted to do was buy them for fifty-nine cents at the grocery store. I learned how to sew my own pajama pants and grow wheat and fold a fitted sheet, and I found out about the rising cost of baseball uniforms. I cheered and listened and learned and smiled and put one foot in front of the other and held my head up high. After all, I was in Rome.

And I truly wanted to be a Roman.

Then one day everything clicked. I was standing in line at the post office when a flyer caught my eye. It was for a gardening club.

Gardening! I thought. *That's something I could do. I've always wanted to start a cutting garden of my own.*

⌒℘

Two weeks later I attended my first meeting. When I first walked in the door, I was a little nervous. I didn't really know anyone, so I sat by myself in the back of the room and listened. I couldn't believe how much the members knew. I took page after page of notes about hydrangeas and how to grow flowers on your porch and how to create a container garden. An hour-long meeting flew by in what felt like minutes.

I left the meeting wearing wings. I couldn't wait to begin, so my notes and I stopped by the gardening center on the way home. Buckets of flowers filled my cart, and visions of container gardens danced in my head as I rushed home to create my masterpiece.

An hour or so later, after I'd finished planting my container garden, I stood back to survey my work. It was amazing.

Just like they said.

I didn't stop there. That next month I planted two more container gardens and marked off a cutting garden in the backyard and bought tomato cages. I felt invincible. Like I could do anything. Like I was ready for another challenge. Like I wanted to try something new.

I'm still not sure why or what or how I decided I was going to take the leap from gardening to cooking, but I did. I reached into my big bag of confidence and decided to put the Ghost of Undercooked Pancakes Past to rest. And right then and there, on an otherwise ordinary Tuesday morning, I decided to cook a roast.

Simple, right? But me? I'd never made a roast in my life, pot or otherwise. My kitchen had seen gas-station pizza and macaroni and cheese and the occasional gourmet hot-dog pie. But a roast? A roast with carrots and potatoes, simmering in a sauce for hours just waiting for dinnertime? That was living high on the hog.

Literally.

I began my journey where all people go when they want to buy a cut of meat or paint a room or get a garden hose or purchase a new set of all-weather tires. It's the pinnacle of meat preparation, the holy grail of all things roast related, the place where humble meat dreams become reality.

Walmart.

I arrived at the store, grabbed a cart, and skipped toward the meat section. I steered the cart past the bread and the peanut butter and the inordinately large section of tea products and rounded the corner to the back of the store.

I had arrived at my destination.

There in front of me stood a giant wall of meat. I paused and stared at the array of choices in absolute consternation. What was all this? There were chuck roasts and round roasts and rib roasts and pork roasts and rump roasts. Which one was best? Which one was right? How in the world was a person supposed to choose?

Especially a frozen-potpie girl just trying to make dinner for the family?

I stood there racking my brain for roasting information, trying to decide what to do next. Should I scrap the whole thing? Should I head home and hang up my oven mitts? Should I forget all this and reintroduce myself to the hot dogs?

At that moment, providence stepped in—in the form of a fellow Walmart-er.

She watched the scene unfold and came to my aid. I explained the meat mountain I was trying to climb, and without so much as a follow-up question, she knew exactly what I needed. She schooled me in everything roast in ten minutes flat, walked me over to the baby carrots and the onion-soup mix, and gave me specific instructions that included words like *easy* and *can't go wrong* and *Crock-Pot*. Then with a smile and well wishes, she sent me on my way.

When I got home, I followed all the directions to the letter. With exquisite care, I lowered the meat into the Crock-Pot. Next, I added water, soup mix, potatoes, onions, and carrots. I left nothing to chance, no stone unturned. Step by step, detail by detail, I prepared my roast.

Then I turned on the Crock-Pot and waited. They say a watched pot never boils, but my Crock-Pot did. Every now and then I would open up the lid and watch the water bubble and the carrots steam as the most delicious smells on the planet wafted out into the kitchen. All that from cooking. Who knew?

It was amazing.

Five hours later, I checked to see if the roast was ready. I opened the lid and peered inside, but it didn't really look done. The meat looked kind of mushy, pinkish in the middle, but dark around the edges. I stuck a fork into the meat to see what it looked like underneath. *Yep, just as I suspected. Still pink.*

Yikes.

What did all that pink mean? Was it cooked? How in the world could a person without any roast experience tell when a roast was done?

I turned off the Crock-Pot and stood in the kitchen with the late-afternoon sunlight dancing across the wood floor. I turned the dilemma over in my mind until suddenly a lightbulb danced over my head. I had it. I knew what to do. I took out the roast, put it on a platter, covered it with foil . . . and drove it to gardening club.

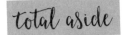

If you're in unfamiliar territory, and you don't know how to take your friendships to the next level, you might try one of these options for breaking the ice: asking questions, introducing a get-to-know-you game, or bringing along a nice piece of meat.

I walked into garden club late and harried and windblown, lugging my foil-covered roast with me as my heels clicked on the white linoleum floor. I placed the platter on the table, took a seat in the back of the room, perched on the edge of my chair, and waited. I didn't want to interrupt the heated discussion on how to trim a crape myrtle tree.

I wish I could tell you I felt great confidence in my decision to take a piece of meat as my garden club date.

But I didn't.

At home, it had all made perfect sense to me. At home, it seemed like a brilliant decision. At home, it was obvious that garden club was full of brilliant, amazing, incredible people who had all the answers, who undoubtedly had extensive experience in cooking and knew all about roasts.

But now that I was at the meeting, a wave of apprehension washed over me. Was this the best way to make a good impression? Was this a wise choice to make friends and influence gardeners? As I sat on my metal folding chair, one thought kept swirling around in my brain over and over and over again: *WHAT WAS I THINKING?*

When at last there was a lull in conversation, I seized the opportunity. I raised my hand and plunged in. "Um, excuse me. I'm really excited about learning how to trim my crape myrtle tree, and you've given me a lot to think about today. I'm new here, and it's really nice to meet all of you." I cleared my throat and continued, "Ladies of garden club, I really need your help."

At that moment, all eyes turned toward the back of the room. As they looked at me and my foil-covered platter, they grinned and nudged each other in anticipation.

"I think she brought cookies," one lady whispered to her neighbor.

With great reverence, I removed the foil from the platter, revealing the large hunk of meat along with a random piece of carrot clinging to it in desperation. My gesture was met with silence and blank stares. My roast seemed to wither under the glare of the overhead fluorescent lights.

You could have heard a piece of aluminum foil drop in the room.

I groaned. What was I thinking? What had I done? This was my brilliant plan. And now? It was sinking like the *Titanic*. Steeling myself, I stayed the course. "Can . . . can . . . um, can you all tell me if this roast is done?" I whispered.

No one spoke. They all just stared at me as if I'd lost my mind. As if the mere act of bringing a roast to garden club defied all reasonable thought and explanation.

Then, from the front of the room, I heard a voice.

Finally, I thought. *An answer. Someone who understands. Someone to guide me through the unknown mysteries of cooking a roast.*

I picked up the platter and made a beeline for my new friend. "Here it is," I said, holding out the platter. "Can you help? Do you think it's done?"

The woman paused, inspected the roast, and then turned to me with a smile. "It's nice to meet you, dear," she said. "I know you're new here, and it's so very nice of you to bring a roast to the meeting." Then she patted my hand and continued, "But you might want to take it home and bring it back later. Cooking class is next week."

At her statement, the room erupted in laughter, and everyone got up to exclaim over the piece of meat that had stopped by to visit garden club. The women gave me advice and cooking times and told me when to layer in vegetables and how to know when the meat was done. Someone brought out sweet tea from the kitchen, and we talked and laughed and told stories and snacked on plates of well-done roast. It was an afternoon to remember.

After garden club, as I drove home down country roads with the sun setting on the horizon, I realized this was what my heart had been hungering for all along. My roast had broken the ice. Through my nervousness and my vulnerability and exposing my weakness, I had opened an unexpected door for friendship.

I felt welcomed.

I felt loved.

I felt like a Roman.

I hummed to myself and sent up a silent prayer of thanks for shared conversations, for a snack of sweet tea and meat slices, for new friends full of laughter and joy, and for the next chapters in our adventure that were just waiting to be written.

And I made sure to wave at every car on the way home.

Garden Club-Inspired Recipe Wall

SUPPLIES

- a large roll of paper
- 1 recipe
  (preferably a family recipe)
- ruler
- pencil
- 1 blank wall with a smooth
  surface *(at least 36 inches wide)*
- level

- 7 packages of alphabet stickers
  approximately 1½ inches tall
  *(Capital letters work best. You
  could also create the project using
  letters created from a vinyl cutting
  machine).*
- patience

1. Start by laying out the recipe on a piece of paper the same size as the wall you are planning to work on. This will show you how many lines you need.

2. Mark off lines for the recipe on the wall. As you work, check your lines with the level to make sure they are straight. Measure from the top and mark off every three inches with a pencil. You can add extra lines at the top if you run out of room at the bottom.

3. On the top line, center the title of the recipe using alphabet stickers.

RECIPE TITLE

4. On the next line, starting on the left-hand side, spell out the word *Ingredients*.

RECIPE TITLE

INGREDIENTS

Continuing on the left-hand side, add each of the ingredients to a new line using the alphabet stickers.

 On a new line, separate the ingredients from the directions with the word *Directions*.

RECIPE TITLE

INGREDIENTS

RECIPE TITLE

INGREDIENTS

DIRECTIONS

7 Add the directions for the recipe line by line, starting from the left-hand side. Continue until you have added the entire recipe to the wall with alphabet stickers.

Note: You can also do this project on the back of a bookcase, a plate rack, a hutch, or anywhere you need a reminder that part of the joy of fitting in is knowing when to stand out.

9

the day goliath met a t. rex

LIFE LESSON #9

When you're facing a problem that seems overwhelming and you don't know where to turn, it may be time to channel your inner dinosaur.

My grandmother once told me that little pitchers have big ears.

At the time, I didn't really understand what she meant, but that didn't matter. She said it so sagely that my five-year-old self took it as the gospel truth. I spent the next few years of childhood tiptoeing and whispering around the pottery on my mother's shelf.

It wasn't until years later, when I had children of my own, that the truth of the statement came home to roost. Our farmhouse was full of little pitchers.

And they never missed a word.

Somehow, without anyone noticing, our family grew and transformed right along with the farmhouse. Month after month, year after year, we made our home our own: putting chairs on the back porch to watch the stars; setting up a laundry room with a washer and dryer in the same location; making a guest room on the top floor, complete with a wall made out of shutters. The house rearranged rooms, smoothed out its floors, sponsored chalkboard parades, and watched as our four children spread their wings, tested the river water, and slowly began to adapt to life in the country.

They explored every inch of our Kentucky acres and wiggled muddy toes in the creek and watched hay being cut in the back pasture and ran like the wind across the rolling farmland. The outdoors was part of our everyday life. My children didn't have to read books about deer and snapping turtles and tortoises and cows and horses and bunnies—these things were all around us.

But moving to a new city, changing schools, and settling into a new house—all of it was challenging. There were new rules to learn and school bus routes to navigate and an entire farming calendar to adjust to. We learned that you had a "come-apart" when you got so excited that you thought you might burst and that sometimes you're just "fixin'" to do something and that when someone tells you they "don't care to help," it means that they really want to chip in. Slowly but surely, one backpack, one hay bale, one tractor at a time, we tried to fit in.

As confident as I was that God had called us to jump, I was nervous. It's one thing to stand next to your minivan and tell the world you're moving. It's another to jump into the challenges of moving four states away. I questioned my decision daily. Would the kids be okay? Would they adjust? Was this really the best decision I could have made as a parent? What if we failed? What if the move was a disaster? What if I let my family down? What if my kids discovered that they were allergic to hay?

This was all so new. It was such a big move for our family. There were new people to meet and new friends to make and a whole new way of life to adjust to. I tried my best to pave the way for them, but I felt so inadequate, so weak, so imperfect.

So helpless.

I put on a brave mom face, but inside I was biting every last fingernail I had. When I drove the kids to school, I was full of encouraging speeches and life-affirming moments, but when I looked in the rearview mirror at the seats full of wide, worried eyes, my bravado would crumble. I wanted to walk those tiny feet to math class and shoot baskets with them in gym class and help their tiny hands write on the board and sit next to them in the cafeteria at lunch.

Just in case no one else did.

I'd spent years preparing my chicks to leave the nest. They could stand in line and write their names and raise their hands to answer questions in class and make little zippers with their mouths when they were supposed to be quiet. All those moments of planning and preparing and discussing were about to be put to the test. This was the moment of truth. I was nervous and scattered and worried and shaking in my yoga pants. And my heart? It kept asking the same question over and over and over again.

Will my chicks fly?

Each of my children is wired uniquely, with a distinct personality. And it has been that way from the moment they arrived in this world. So it came as no surprise that each one responded to the move so differently.

Denton, my oldest child, is my cheerful giver. My geography representative. My future Nobel Prize candidate. He's funny and smart and wise beyond his years, and when he laughs, the world can't help but join in. He was the most attached to Dallas, and he reluctantly packed up his memories and experiences of our old home and brought them with him on our journey. At first I wondered how well he'd adapt. But two weeks after we arrived, he joined the academic team and never looked back.

His decorating choices reflected his personality too. This detail-oriented child of mine planned every last nook and cranny of his room. There was a giant mural that covered one wall and globes and bulletin boards for notes and pictures and a sign with pi on it.

And I'm not talking about the kind you eat. I'm talking about the kind you memorize the first thirty-two digits of.

Zachary, my middle child, is my warrior. My mountain climber. My mom humbler. My dinosaur in training.

And my heart?
It kept asking the
same question over
and over and over
again. Will my
chicks fly?

Zack arrived ready to take on our little town in the bluegrass. He never looked back—not for a moment. He joined the basketball team and the baseball team and played third base like he was in the major leagues. He ran faster and dove harder than anyone, and he stuck out his tongue between his teeth in concentration when he stepped up to the plate.

And got more grass stains on his pants than the rest of the team combined.

My brother once created a book for Zack in which he superimposed pictures of Zack riding pterodactyls and stegosauruses and velociraptors on every page. Zack is sixteen now. I think he still believes that book is true.

His room was all about sports and the little boys who love them. It was red and white and navy, with bookshelves full of tickets and trophies and ripped baseballs and pieces of wood he'd collected on his adventures in the woods. He acted like he was grown and tough and ready to leave home with nothing but a knapsack. But he still kept his trusty stuffed zebra named Zorro tucked away for rough days when he needed him.

I think of all my children, the twins adapted best to the move. After all, they had each other. It was like getting to visit a new planet and bringing along your best friend for the rocket ride.

Westleigh is the organizer, the Post-it note writer, the sparkler, the one who keeps us on track and makes sure the pan of brownies is divided up into equal shares. She's my firstborn daughter. My trailblazer. My future red lipstick wearer. My fearless pastry slicer.

Whitney, my baby, is the family peacemaker, the keeper of secrets, the dog's champion. She'd give you her last bite of sandwich, listen attentively to every word of your stories, braid your hair, and ask you if you love Jesus. Her smile can brighten even the darkest of gray skies, and she remembers every birthday in the history of birthdays. She's my tenderhearted believer. My champion for the less fortunate. My heart melter.

When it was time to decorate their room, the twins were full of opinions and teacups. They wanted bright colors and flowers and lamps that twinkled and sparkled with extra glitter on top. We decorated the room with matching monogrammed beds and a colorful orange-and-fuchsia rug that covered the floor. In that room, they taught lessons to an entire classroom of dolls and elephants and turtles and a bunny with glasses, and tea was served promptly at two o'clock every afternoon.

Hats required.

These were our children, our people, our troop, our band of merry pitchers.

⌒ℛℴ

Just a few weeks into the school year, Zack ran into the house and tossed his backpack on the floor with all the angst and despair a brand-new first grader could muster.

"Mom, you're not going to believe it," he said, eyes blazing. "We have a bully."

"A bully?" I repeated. "Really? In first grade?"

"Yes. A bully," he repeated. "And he's big and strong and mean. And he pushes kids down on the playground."

Day after day, he repeated a version of the same story. As the stories continued, the legend of the bully grew to almost epic proportions. My son would talk about how the bully took kids' lunches, pushed his way to the head of the line, and made mean faces at the rest of the class. One day he reported that the bully had pulled a girl's hair in math class and pretended to punch someone and stole someone's quarter in the lunchroom.

Just when the bully news couldn't get any worse, one of the teachers discovered that someone had written not-very-nice words on the bathroom walls. No one confessed. No one told the teacher who had done such a despicable act. But everyone knew.

It was the bully.

Like a creature from an old-school horror movie, he was the toughest of the tough. The scariest of the scary. The very meanest of the mean.

As a mom, I found it all a little overwhelming. I dreaded those bully stories. What would he do next? Why didn't anyone address the problem at school? I wanted to call the office myself, but I was worried. We were new to the area. Should I make waves? Should I talk to the teacher? Should I call and make an appointment with the principal?

Zack begged me not to say anything. "You'll only make it worse, Mom," he said. "He'll know I told, and then he might take my quarter next."

Right about when I couldn't take it anymore, when I was ready to call in the National Guard, when I was ready to write Dear Abby a long letter about bullies and the moms who don't like them very much, when I was ready to pull out every last hair from the top of my head . . . it stopped.

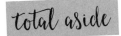

We are wired as moms to protect our children using whatever we have in our arsenal. Here in Kentucky, we have horses. I have no idea how to saddle up, but don't think the idea of riding in on a white horse didn't cross my mind.

From that day forward, I never heard another bully story. All the tales and escapades and struggles and lunch taking simply disappeared. All those mean faces? All that questionable bathroom writing? All that hair pulling?

Not. Another. Word.

To say I was curious was an understatement. What had happened? What had changed overnight? What would be the next chapter in the chronicles of first grade with a bully?

The next week, when Zack arrived home from school cheerfully discussing math class and who sat by whom and laughing about a funny story that the teacher told to the class, I decided I couldn't take it anymore.

I had to know.

"Whatever happened to that bully?" I asked casually. "You never really talk about him anymore. Is he still around?"

My son stared at me blankly.

"The bully?" he said. "Oh. I kind of forgot about him. He's fine. He's not really bothering anyone anymore."

I couldn't believe it. It was such a miraculous change. Dumbfounded, I asked, "Did he move? Did he change schools?"

Zack grinned at me from across the table.

"You're not going to believe it, Mom. Last week he came up to me on the playground. He was glaring at me with really mean eyes and making an ugly face at me and clenching his fists. He was coming closer and closer, and I was so scared." He stopped and reached for a drink of milk.

Panicked, I prompted, "And then? What happened next? What happened after he came up to you? Did you tell the teacher?"

"Nope." He smiled the most wonderful toothless grin I'd ever seen. "I just couldn't take it anymore. I was done with all that bullying." He shrugged and munched on a cookie. "So I looked him in the face and turned into a tyrannosaurus rex. I put my claws in the air, threw back my head, and growled the loudest growl I could."

I laughed in relief. "You turned into a T. rex?"

"Yep!" Zack shook a claw in the air for emphasis. "And his face got all red and scared, and he ran away. And guess what? He hasn't bothered anyone since."

My son had faced down Goliath with God and the strength of a thousand dinosaurs.

A little child will lead them.

Why had I worried? Why had I doubted? Why had I wasted a moment on things that were out of my control? This was all part of God's plan. He knew. He understood. He had led us to the promised land, and he was making our path straight.

All we needed to do was put our faith in him. I hit my knees and sent a silent prayer of thanks. Gratitude washed over me as I thanked him for the unexpected blessings of our jump. I rejoiced over the joy of the journey and broken farmhouses that could be a testimony and the patience learned from driving behind a piece of oversized farm equipment and bullies who had finally met their match.

And for the little pitchers who had been listening all along.

Display-Your-Inner-Tyrannosaurus Pillow

SUPPLIES

+ scissors
+ 1 small canvas drop cloth
+ sewing machine
+ 1 spool matching or contrasting thread
+ iron
+ printer
+ printer paper
+ pencil
+ 1 sheet graphite paper
+ ½ yard of contrasting fabric for the monogram
+ sewing needle
+ 1 pillow form insert (20 inches by 20 inches)
+ 1 bottle fabric glue (if you want to make it no-sew)

1 Cut two squares out of the drop cloth that measure 21 inches by 21 inches each.

2 Place the two pieces (which will be the sides of the pillow) on top of each other.

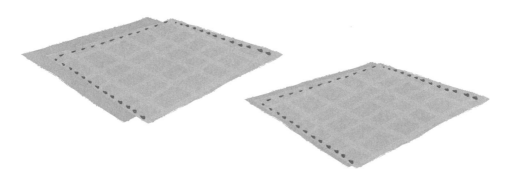

3 Using the sewing machine, sew the squares together. The seam should be ½ inch from the edge. Backstitch approximately two inches at the beginning and end to prevent ripping when you insert the pillow form. Leave a wide opening at one end of the squares to insert the pillow.

4 Turn the sewn squares right side out and poke out the corners. Iron the pillow cover flat.

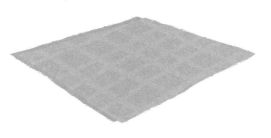

5 Choose a font for a monogram, and print it out on your printer. The monogram should be at least 7 inches tall.

6 Using a pencil and the graphite paper, trace the monogram onto the contrasting fabric. Cut out the monogram just inside the traced lines.

7 Stitch the monogram onto the pillow cover with a needle and thread.

8 Insert the pillow form into the pillow cover. Stitch the pillow closed.

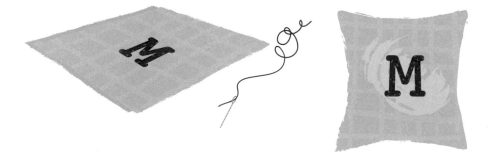

9 Fluff the pillow and toss it onto the couch. You can even karate chop it the next time you need to channel your inner dinosaur.

Note: If you want a no-sew option, follow steps 5 and 6, glue the fabric monogram onto a premade pillow cover, and zip in a pillow insert.

10

my achilles hips

LIFE LESSON #10

*Your heaviest burden may not be
the one people can see. It may be
the one your heart is carrying.*

I t was all so perfect.

Everything. The farmhouse was almost finished. Our family was fitting into the community, and the kids were doing well in school. My husband's new job as a full-time pharmacist was fulfilling and enriching and everything he'd hoped it would be. My blog, called *Thistlewood Farms* after our never-ending battle with thistles on our property, had evolved into a full-time business. I'd started it to document the house renovations and my DIY projects. My readership started with my mother, my brother, and my cousin's cousin twice removed. But over time the blog grew, and against all odds, I somehow managed to develop a following of people I wasn't related to.

My new job as a blogger also opened opportunities to partner with some incredible companies. I had a husband I loved, a home I wanted to marry, happy and healthy children, and acres of bluegrass in the country. From the outside looking in, my life looked like a storybook.

If my life were the script of a Hallmark movie, I couldn't have written it any better.

But if you looked closer, if you peeled back the pages of the script and dug a little deeper into my heart, you'd know. You'd see that I was battling a demon with a grip so tight on me it left me weary and broken.

That demon? It was my struggle with my weight.

Truthfully, I'd always been a little heavy. The kind of heavy that comes with its own set of names, like chubby or pleasingly plump or stocky or tubby or chunky.

Or fluffy.

When I was younger, I remember overhearing a friend of the

family whispering it to my mother. They stood in the kitchen, watching me as I slouched in a chair after school, dipping Oreos in milk.

"Maybe she'll grow taller," I overheard her say in low undertones to my mother. "She's just got a little bit of extra weight on her. It's actually kind of cute. She's not fat. She's just fluffy."

As I listened to their hushed conversation, I wanted to scream at them at the top of my lungs. I wanted to shout so loud my voice could be heard across seven counties. I wanted to yell, "I'm right here. I hear you, and I'm NOT FLUFFY."

But I didn't. I didn't say a single word. Instead, I acted like I couldn't hear them talking about me. I ignored it all and pushed the hurt deep inside, layering it on top of frustration and shame.

And slowly dipped another Oreo.

Throughout my high school years, I continued to struggle with my weight, but I never let it hold me back. I had lots of friends, ran for student council, got good grades, and never missed a football game. I even tried out to be our high school's mascot.

total aside

Our school's mascot was the lion. At tryouts, I planned an entire routine that featured a big growl and a somersault at the end. But somehow, I ended up rolling into the judges' table instead. I didn't get chosen to be the mascot, but I was voted "most likely to cheer for the team from the sidelines."

I was the funny one. The life of the party. The center of attention. I laughed harder and sang louder and danced faster than anyone else in the room.

It wasn't that I didn't know I was heavy. I simply told myself I'd worry about it tomorrow. Tomorrow I'd go on a diet. Tomorrow I'd start a new exercise program. Tomorrow I'd drink eight glasses of water a day and wear leg warmers and do leg lifts and go all Jane Fonda. Tomorrow I'd be skinny and wear size eight jeans and add carrots to my favorite-foods list.

Except.

Except tomorrow never came.

As I grew older, *diet* became my middle name. I'd lose weight and gain it back and repeat the same pattern over and over and over again. I was always on the lookout for a new eating plan.

I tried everything. One week I'd eat nothing but vegetables and fruit. The next week I'd stick with protein. I experimented with high-fat diets and low-fat diets and meal plans without sugar and menus that were high in fiber. The odder the diet sounded, the more convinced I was that it was going to work.

I spent my life chasing skinny.

Then, when I was a sophomore in college, I started dating Denton. He was understanding and kind and accepting, with twinkling brown eyes and big muscles and a smile that made me melt from across the room. My favorite thing about him? He loved me exactly the way I was. He never questioned my weight or tried to change me. And he never called me fluffy.

He simply called me beautiful.

We got married and moved to San Diego, where he was stationed with the Navy. Several months later, in the midst of the Persian Gulf War, Denton's ship was called up for an overseas mission. After we'd been married for one year, two weeks, and four days, he came home and announced that he was leaving for seven months.

What?

I couldn't believe it. Didn't the United States government understand? We were newlyweds. We were just getting to know each other. I clung to Denton and asked if he could talk to someone about this little mix-up. I patiently explained that this wasn't in the script. In all the romantic comedies I'd watched, no one went out to sea for seven months. He simply smiled at me with those twinkling eyes, kissed me, and told me I would be all right.

Two weeks later, he was gone.

At first I cried. Then I got mad. Then I pouted. Then I sat on the couch for days on end, eating brownie sundaes and watching old episodes of *90210*. And somewhere between Brandon and Brenda arriving at the new high school and Kelly and Steve breaking up and getting back together, I got inspired.

Tomorrow had finally arrived.

Over the next seven months I turned off the television and traded brownie sundaes for broccoli and grilled chicken. I started running and became the leg-lift champion of the West Coast. I was intense. I was on fire. I was driven. I chased tomorrow with single-minded purpose and the hope and dream and goal of losing forty pounds.

And I did.

The week before my husband arrived home, I started preparing for the reunion. I highlighted my hair, waxed my eyebrows, and painted my new acrylic nails the most beautiful shade of red the world had ever seen. I spent hours shopping for the perfect meet-your-husband-when-he-arrives-home-after-you've-lost-forty-pounds outfit.

I found just the right dress tucked at the back of the clearance rack. It was a rich shade of purple, with slits cut down to here and sliced up to here. I added matching purple heels and earrings that sparkled and danced when I walked. Day after day, I practiced different poses in my new outfit in front of the mirror and discovered that if I held in my stomach, put my hand on my hip, turned slightly to the right, crossed my legs and made a fish face, I looked even skinnier.

It was the perfect pose.

At last it was time to meet my sailor. He was flying home early from his deployment into LAX. I arrived at the airport early and looked around until I found the skinniest location in the room: a stand-alone pillar next to the coffee machine. I parked myself there in my purple dress, standing quietly with my hand on my hip, my stomach tight, and wearing my best fish face to accentuate my newly skinny cheekbones.

Posing and waiting.

Slowly the sailors disembarked. I peered through the sea of white uniforms, searching impatiently for Denton's face. At last, I saw him. My heart raced a million miles a minute as I stood and stared, taking in his dimples, brown eyes, and chiseled features.

Without skipping a beat, I re-struck the pose.

The crowd parted, and I could see him in the distance, his eyes scanning the crowd. I willed him to look in my direction and see the changes I'd made and the weight I'd lost and my incredible purple dress. I closed my eyes and imagined him sweeping me into his arms. This was it. This was my moment. The excitement built as he came closer and closer and closer.

And walked right past me.

He hadn't even recognized me!

He didn't see me until I called his name, broke my perfect pose, and ran to the place I'd dreamed of for seven long, self-improving months.

Right into his arms.

total aside

You know the part in Hallmark movies where the guy finally gets the girl, and he wraps her in his arms and hugs her tight, and their eyes meet, and you wonder if it's really as amazing as it looks? It is.

I wish this story ended right here with me wearing a purple dress and kissing forty pounds good-bye and riding off into the sunset in the arms of a sailor. But it doesn't. Not even close. Those forty pounds came back with a vengeance and brought some friends along for the ride. It was a never-ending battle.

And I was losing the war.

Food became my comfort. Over the course of giving birth to four children, moving from state to state, making career changes, getting a master's degree, and facing the everyday challenges of life, food was my companion. It became my friend, my confidant, and my protector. It was there for me on days when I was flying high and needed to celebrate, and it was there to make me feel better when I was feeling frustrated and hurt.

Food was constant. It was faithful. It showed up and healed my wounds and dusted me off and gave me the confidence to face another day.

Over time, the pounds continued to pack on. I wore that weight like a shield of armor to protect my heart from getting bruised. I hid in the background whenever anyone took pictures. I embraced leggings as a fashion choice because they made me feel skinnier. I worried about fitting into movie seats. I was scared the bar wouldn't close when I went on rides at the amusement park.

I coped by making jokes about my weight. I wanted everyone to think I was okay with it. That it was a little thing. That it meant nothing to me.

But it meant everything.

When we moved to Kentucky, I was at my heaviest. The stress of the move and the new environment and all the life changes made me cling to my old friend, food, even more tightly. I tried to lose the weight. Truly. I'd eat broccoli and spinach for a couple of days and exercise like I was a contestant on a reality show. But at the first sign of trouble or distress, I'd dive headfirst into a brownie sundae.

I decided I needed a purpose, a new focus, a distraction from all those carbohydrates. Starting the blog turned out to be a lifesaver.

The me of today
is so much
better than the
me of tomorrow.

I found an online community where I belonged, where I fit in. I shared about our home and detailed the renovations. I told stories and created projects and painted rooms and added molding and made treasures out of trash. I created pumpkins out of twigs and tassels out of faucet heads and transoms out of windows, and along the way, I discovered something amazing.

Online everyone is skinny.

On the blog, my hair always had the best day ever. At Thistlewood, my husband was always clever and funny, the children were always well-behaved and said the cutest things, the house was always clean, and I always walked around in three-inch heels and size eight velvet pants. Online, I wore the cutest outfits, my earrings always dazzled, and my red lipstick was perfectly applied.

Until.

Until one day when real life and the blog intersected.

I was asked to attend a real-life event that would include hundreds of people from my online niche. I'd meet other bloggers and greet people and interact with an audience and a stage and a microphone. There would be photographers and cameras, and the event would be recorded for posterity, along with me and all those extra pounds.

I balked.

I couldn't do it. I couldn't go. If I showed up, everyone would know. Everyone would see the person behind the blog and realize no one was wearing size eight velvet anything. So I took the coward's way out. I made up an elaborate excuse, explained that I was honored and flattered but that I had something else going on and I'd have to miss it.

And then I hid.

I went all ostrich and ducked my head in the sand. I'm not proud of it. Not even a little. The rubber met the road, and I took a detour. At that moment, I came face-to-face with the reality of how much my weight controlled my life. I felt helpless and unworthy and ugly and fluffy to the tenth power.

Then the most amazing thing happened.

On the afternoon of the event that went on without me, when I was sobbing and lying on my bed, God used all that ugliness and self-doubt for his glory. In the midnight of that moment, he whispered the words I had been longing to hear, straight to my heart.

You are loved.

I can't accept it, I thought. *I don't deserve it.*

You are worthy.

Why, Lord? Who am I?

You are a daughter of the King.

As those words of healing and acceptance washed over me, I felt the burden I was carrying melt away. I felt the guilt and the pain and the hurt lift from me. I glimpsed the joy beyond the curtain that was mine for the taking, and in that glorious, amazing moment, something in my heart shifted.

In the pain of that moment, God reminded me, ever so gently, that I wasn't defined by a number on a scale or a pixelated image on the screen or the size on the tag of my fashion leggings. I was valuable. I had worth. I was precious and adored and loved because I was created in his image.

Simply because I was his.

I didn't have to lose weight to gain his favor. The power that food had over me? It wasn't of him. Food could never fill the deep need for comfort and acceptance and approval inside me. Only God could.

⟋⟋

Truthfully, my new weight-loss journey hasn't always been easy. I wish I could put on an astronaut suit and run around my house a couple of times and the pounds would disappear like magic. But those days of wishing for quick fixes are gone. I've left behind the fads and started eating healthy and making better choices and exercising more. I'm halfway to my goal weight now, but even with all the progress, the journey ahead seems overwhelming at times. Sometimes the weight we carry in our minds is so much harder to shed than the pounds on the scale. There are days when I feel like I'm carrying the heaviness of the world on my shoulders.

Literally.

But I'm learning. I'm learning that exercise brings you sunshine and that water tastes better than a Diet Coke ever could. I'm learning that you don't always have to add sugar to the guest list. I'm learning that the me of today is so much better than the me of tomorrow. Every day I'm loving this self I've been given a little more, and I'm fearing the weight a little less.

I'm still challenged. I still have miles to go. There are still days when the clouds roll in and the storms gather on the horizon and the pitfalls stretch out before me, but now it's different. Instead of reaching into the pantry, instead of filling my emptiness with food, instead of rolling back into the darkness, I remember that still, small voice, put down the burden I've been carrying, and adjust my crown.

The "I Am Amazing" Mirror

+ saw
+ 1 piece plywood
  (2 feet by 4 feet)
+ 1 piece of mirrored glass
  (approximately 12 inches by
  24 inches)
+ 4 pieces reclaimed wood
  (4 inches wide)

+ 1 bottle wood glue
+ letters spelling out
  "I Am Amazing"
  (You can cut these out on
  a vinyl cutter or use stickers
  to spell out the words.)

Cut the piece of plywood large enough that there will be a 4-inch border around the mirror.

② Cut the reclaimed wood to create a frame for the mirror. Two short pieces will be used for the top and bottom. Two longer pieces will be used for the sides.

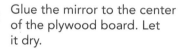

③ Glue the mirror to the center of the plywood board. Let it dry.

④ Place the longer pieces of wood next to the sides of the mirror and the shorter pieces of wood next to the top and bottom of the mirror, and glue them in place. Let them dry.

5 Arrange the vinyl cutout letters at the top of the mirror, and glue them in place.

6 Hang up the mirror as a reminder of the incredible, amazing, accepted, unique individual you are. Then take on the day.

11

flooded with possibilities

LIFE LESSON #11

When the river is rising and sandbagging is in your future, it's time to call a friend. Or a town.

used to think natural disasters happened only on television. As I flipped through the channels, I'd see tornadoes and hurricanes and earthquakes and tsunamis that were larger than life on our tiny television screen. Glued to the news from the comfort of my living room, I'd watch as meteorologists stood in yellow rain slickers or hooded fleece-lined parkas, turning about in the rain or snow or wind. It all seemed so surreal. So otherworldly. So happening-somewhere-else.

Until.

Until I moved to the country.

All of a sudden I was Laura Ingalls, facing down the blizzard and holding tight to Carrie and Mary in a house without electricity while Pa felt his way along a rope to feed the cows. In the years since my family and I crossed the plains and the fields and the meadows and the Mississippi River to land in the beautiful bluegrass of Kentucky, we've experienced an ice storm that shut down the entire town and left us without electricity for seventeen days. We've watched as hail the size of golf balls peppered the countryside. We've had a tornado that ripped off part of our roof and a herculean thunderstorm that tossed almost three feet of water into our yard and flooded our cars.

But the most powerful natural disaster of all? The one that has been written about in poems and odes and all the missing third verses of hymns everywhere? The one that will be passed down from generation to generation in hushed tones and whispers? The one that brought me to my knees and forced me to take a river's name in vain?

The flood of 2010.

We live in an area where two rivers meet and two other rivers shake hands and hang out. Back when we first thought about moving to Kentucky, we stood on the banks of one of those rivers and heard God whispering to our hearts. Lulled by the beauty of the country-side and the rivers that flowed along, dotted with birds and fishing boats, I somehow missed part of that whispered conversation. No one mentioned that a rolling, idyllic, peaceful river doesn't always stay where it's supposed to. No one mentioned rising waters or sand-bags or eroding riverbanks. No one bothered to tell me that rivers are just like two-year-olds.

Both can throw a pretty mean tantrum.

I first heard a hint of the impending flood while I was driving down the interstate in the rain. "The water is rising after getting more rain than expected this week," the scratchy voice of the news-caster blared out over the radio. "All the gates of the dam are being opened." The constant refrain, along with the swish of the wipers on my windshield, was, "Possible flooding. Possible flooding."

No big deal, I thought. *It's just a little water. It always rains in April.* As I turned toward home, I peered out through the buckets of water that were cascading across my windshield.

The water didn't stop.

Not for a minute. Not for a second. Every day the skies around us opened up and poured torrential rain across the county. We are almost completely surrounded by rivers and streams and creeks and lakes that were rising higher by the minute. I'd look out through the curtains in the living room, watch the dark clouds fill with rain, and cling desperately to the promise God made to Noah. Those rising waters threatened everything we had built. Literally. Our home. Our business. The two-story tree house in the backyard. A flood would wash everything away, including our life savings.

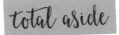

I have a love/hate relationship with the song about Noah and the arky arky. When I was growing up, my mother sang a slightly off-key version to us every morning to wake us up. She was always rising us and shining us, and while I loved to hear her sing, I just wanted to give God some glory a little later in the day.

As the river inched higher and higher, our little community started making plans. We had meetings about the river and the weather forecast and the potential for flooding. The initial strategy was to place a few sandbags in the low spots by the river. Eventually, as the waters continued to rise, we decided to create a wall of sandbags seven city blocks wide.

If you've never moved from the city to a country town on the edge of a river about to flood and worked a sandbag location before, here's a quick primer on how the process works. Dump trucks of sand are brought in to load enormous sandbag-filling machines, which have funnels located at the bottom. To fill a single sandbag, you hold a tightly woven plastic bag under the machine. The operator then opens the lever to allow sand to trickle into your bag. Once the bag is full, you drag it away, tie it off, and throw it into a truck to be driven to the sandbag wall down by the river.

Each of us had a job in the sandbag-a-palooza of 2010. I was too short to lift the bags into the truck, too uncoordinated to tie off the bag, and too un-mechanical to work the lever.

Instead, I became a truck driver.

Day after day I drove the truck from one end of town to the other. The work was never ending. It was stressful and overwhelming and dirty and exhausting. I'd pull up and help lug the bags out to the truck. Then I'd pick up the empty bags and start the whole process over again.

It was all so hard. I just wanted the whole thing to end. I wanted to tell all the sandbags to take a hike. I wanted to go all Scarlett O'Hara and shake my fist at the sky. Instead, I did the only thing that a truck-driving, sandbag-lugging, stressed-out person can do in the middle of a crisis.

I went to a yard sale.

I know it was the middle of a flood. I understand that hauling sandbags to save the town should have been my first priority. But I couldn't help it. I'd been sandbagging for four days straight in ripped jeans, a dusty Texas Longhorns sweatshirt, a glittery rubber band, and hair that hadn't seen shampoo or a brush for over a week, so I simply couldn't turn away when I glimpsed the siren song of all siren songs.

A sign for a multifamily yard sale.

I'm still not sure why someone decided to have a yard sale in the middle of a flood, but that minor detail was lost on me when I pulled up to the house. Treasures were scattered across the lawn like jewels in a crown. The heavens opened—but this time, instead of rain, it was angels singing a heavenly chorus. Those voices rang out in sweet harmony while birds chirped and flower petals danced.

Almost immediately after I pulled in, I saw it. The exact thing I had no idea I'd been looking for. In the middle of dishes and pot racks and old magazines and a set of truck tires sat the most amazing farmhouse table I'd ever seen.

It had my name written all over it.

I leaped from the cab and strolled over to the table as casually as I could. Like I wasn't in the slightest of hurries. Like I had all the time in the world. Like I wasn't interested in this table or how much it cost or even if anyone else wanted to buy it.

Perfect yard sale strategy.

As I strolled across the yard, I picked up a set of ice trays and examined them. Then I walked over to another table, stacking and unstacking a set of plastic bins and giving a vintage coffee crate another look. Coffee crates make great organizers, holding an endless supply of possibilities. I've picked them up before for under ten dollars and used them to make organizers for my platters in the kitchen.

But that day I had other yard sale fish to fry. I walked past the crate and made my way closer and closer to that farmhouse find. Then, in the most offhand, nonchalant voice I could muster, I inquired how much the table was.

The woman running the yard sale looked me up and down as I stood there in all my glory, with my seven-day hair, torn jeans, and sand-covered sweatshirt. Maybe it was the outfit. Maybe she felt sorry for me. Maybe it had been a rough day at the yard sale. Or maybe she thought I looked like a person who might give a farm-house table a good home.

Whatever the motivation, the words that came out of her mouth made me gasp.

"That table is twenty-five dollars," she said gruffly.

I stared at her, speechless. My mouth opened and shut and opened again without squeezing out a single word.

Twenty-five dollars? I asked myself. *Did I hear her correctly? Twenty-five dollars for this glorious, wonderful bit of farmhouse joy? Am I in an alternate universe?*

Instinctively, my hands tightened on the top of the table. I had to have it. I couldn't let it go. Panicked, I looked around to make sure no one else had heard this conversation. *Get ahold of yourself, KariAnne,* I told myself sternly.

total aside

When shopping at yard sales, your best friend is a pitiful outfit. Un-iron your T-shirt. Add a few rips to your jeans. Wear flip-flops with a broken strap. Don't dress for success, and the world can be yours for only a quarter.

In that moment, as I prepared to accept her offer, something incredible happened. The yard sale proprietor took my blank stare, my lack of conversation, and my convulsive grip on her furniture as my attempt at negotiation.

And lowered the price.

"Okay," she said with a sigh. "If you give me twenty dollars, it's yours."

Well, if you insist . . .

I grabbed a twenty from the pocket of my ripped jeans, pushed the sandbags aside, and loaded the table into the truck. I turned the corner and waved good-bye to the yard sale. As I drove away, smiling gleefully, I heard a sweet sound coming across the cornfields.

It was the angels, starting a second verse.

The river continued to rise.

It was the battle of the ages. A classic struggle of man versus nature. We'd fill the sandbags and build the wall as fast as we could, but the water would meet us at every turn. Like generations before us, we faced the river with courage and strength and single-minded purpose. Crews worked day and night stacking the sandbags by the river.

The sandbag wall was positioned on a steep incline near a road facing the river. Normally the river flowed ten to fifteen feet below the edge of the road, but now the water lapped at the edges of the pavement. At first, we stacked the bags five bags high. But the river continued to rise, pounding against the wall of sandbags. So a sixth layer was added, and then a seventh and an eighth. Finally, we placed one last layer of plastic bags filled with sand atop the wall.

It was an impressive sight. A community had come together with single-minded purpose and the strength of a thousand men and women to defend our homes against a mighty foe. Volunteers packed up the houses in town and prepared shelters for those who had been displaced by the rising river.

The biggest concern for our family was that if the sandbag wall broke, our pharmacy would flood. Everything—the fixtures, the medicine, the gift items, the Formica countertops—would be gone. Denton and I wanted to add another layer of sandbag wall around the business to protect it, but there were only two of us. To our amazement, the community stepped in to help. Residents rallied around all the businesses in town, including our pharmacy, adding even more sandbags around individual buildings to try to brace against the floodwaters.

And still the river continued to rise.

After five long, teary-eyed, prayer-filled days, we heard reports that the inevitable was going to happen. The meteorologists predicted that the river would crest at levels above our sandbag wall. Our seemingly insurmountable wall of sand wouldn't be able to hold back the waters any longer. Hundreds of homes would be flooded, the main street would be underwater, and dozens of businesses would have to close their doors. The destruction that would be left behind—mold, mildew, rotted drywall, and structural damage—would destroy our town. For all intents and purposes, our town was lost.

It was over. The river had won.

The whole town was heartbroken. All that effort. All those sandbags. All those days of messy buns and seven-day hair and torn jeans and dusty sweatshirts.

Around four o'clock the town was evacuated, and the National Guard was called in. Our family piled into our minivan and headed thirty miles away to my sister's home in another town on higher

But in the end?
Truly, all
we needed was
a little faith.

ground. As we headed west, I took one final glimpse in the rear-view mirror at the town we now knew as home. Was this it? Was it over? Were our best-laid plans about to be wiped out with the floodwaters?

Collectively we held our breath and kept our eyes glued to the television. The six o'clock news foretold the worst. The river was cresting five hundred feet from our town and our business. Our family gathered for prayer in the living room of my sister's house and braced for the devastation to come.

As I lay in the guest-room bed that night sobbing, clinging to prayer and Scripture and a worn, fluffy snowflake blanket, I was haunted by that last glimpse of our tiny town. I tried to remind myself that God was listening. I tried to tell myself that God doesn't always answer prayers in the way we expect him to. I thought about other times and other crossroads, some of which hadn't ended the way I'd prayed for.

Like the time I had asked for healing for my grandmother. She suffered from a lengthy illness that had caused her considerable pain. My grandmother was my steady rock, my four-foot-ten-inch Scrabble opponent, my Bible-story teacher, my listening ear, and my favorite Walmart shopping companion. Without her I would be lost.

I spent hours on my knees, with tears streaming down my face, seeking answers and begging for renewed health. But my grandmother never recovered. One day, with little warning, she slipped away from us, and I was left asking why. Why didn't God listen to my prayers? Why didn't he hear me?

What if God didn't answer this prayer like I wanted either?

What if there wasn't a happily-ever-after?

What if this was the end of our journey?

Then, in the quiet of the night, those tender words of encouragement from that moment in the church pew came rushing back.

Trust in me.

Lean not on your own understanding.

I will make your paths straight.

Sweet words of reassurance. Sweeter still because of the darkness of the hour and the uncertainty of what lay ahead. I grabbed on to every letter of every phrase and held on tight. Peace washed over me as I gathered up the burdens I was carrying—just like I'd carried all those sandbags—and laid them down before the only one who had power over the wind and the waves. Then I drifted off to sleep to these words of comfort from Matthew 11:28-30: "Come to me, all you who are weary and burdened, and I will give you rest. Take my yoke upon you and learn from me, for I am gentle and humble in heart, and you will find rest for your souls. For my yoke is easy and my burden is light."

The buzzing of the alarm clock woke us early the next morning. We threw on clothes, hopped into the car, and drove to the riverfront, fearful of what lay ahead of us. Had the wall held back the water? Had the town flooded? Was our business gone? Was our home gone?

Was life as we knew it forever changed?

We crested the hill, and there before us lay the town.

Untouched.

Unflooded.

Unscathed.

Laughter danced across the surface of the river as I took in the sight of the houses and roads and neighborhoods and businesses, all standing like a picture from a storybook in the early morning sunlight. Everything was just as we'd left it. The town was safe. And the wall? That glorious, wonderful, amazing, incredible, nine-bag-high wall of sand?

It stood gleaming in the sun, a testament to the power of perseverance. A symbol of a town and a people who came together with relentless stubbornness, fearless tenacity, and unsinkable faith in the face of adversity. It stood as proof that all the hard work and intense struggle had not been in vain.

The river eventually retreated. The National Guard left, and everyone returned to their streets and sidewalks and homes and businesses. The town lived to tell the story of how determination and grit and resolve and courage had all played a part.

But in the end? Truly, all we needed was a little faith.

No larger than a grain of sand.

DIY Coffee Crate Possibility Holders

SUPPLIES

+ 1 oversized coffee crate
+ saw
+ 100-grit sandpaper
+ hammer

+ nails
+ 1 piece plywood
  (cut into 2 1-yard strips)

1 Shop at yard sales (preferably not in the middle of sandbagging) for a vintage coffee crate.

2 Cut the coffee crate in half, preserving the two long sides with writing on them.

3 Cut each of the halves of the crate in half, again preserving the long sides with writing on them so that you have four slices.

4 Set aside the two pieces with writing on the outside (the original front and back of the crate). These will be your two wall pockets.

5 Take the two remaining slices and pry apart the boards from them.

6 Sand off any rough edges with 100-grit sandpaper.

7 Nail the pried-off boards to the back of the two pieces you set aside, creating two oversized wall pockets.

8 Nail additional strips of plywood to the back for added stability. Reinforce the bottom with plywood if necessary.

9 Hang your wall pockets on the wall and fill them with platters, dishes, maps, place mats, or even wrapping paper. The possibilities are endless.

12

if you blink,
you'll miss the french fries

LIFE LESSON #12

*When you look back on the journey,
you discover that the extraordinary
parts of life are often found in
the most ordinary of moments.*

If you live in Texas for any length of time, you quickly learn that the soil is not your friend. It's hard and dry and crumbly and not conducive to growing anything but tumbleweeds and more dirt. In the Lone Star State, they have to talk cacti into visiting.

When we purchased our old home in Dallas, I wasn't about to let that dirt define me. I wanted an English garden full of lilacs and roses and azaleas and hydrangeas. Everyone laughed. They told me it could never be done.

"Lilacs? Hydrangeas?" they said in disbelief. "No one grows hydrangeas here. You're wasting your time. Try prairie grass instead."

I shook my head, smiled to myself, and dug my heels into the dirt.

Literally.

I was determined to make this work, so I read and planned and plotted and found out how to amend the soil. I added nutrients and compost and peat and sand, and I tilled the dirt until it was rich and fertile. I dug a hole deep in the earth to give the roots room to spread, and then, slowly and tenderly, I placed a tiny hydrangea plant into the ground.

And waited.

Over the days and weeks that followed, I watered and trimmed and encouraged and stood watch over my hydrangea plant. Finally, one day I saw it—the tiniest of flowers. It wasn't much, just a cluster of miniature green dots. But the petals grew and stretched, and one day those green dots blossomed into a beautiful flower.

That hydrangea eventually grew to become a part of me. A testament to survival. A success story of belief and planning and care in the face of overwhelming odds. I couldn't bear to leave it behind. So when we headed to Kentucky, I brought one of the plants along for the journey.

A new beginning.

I wasn't worried about replanting the flowering bush. Kentucky soil is much more welcoming than the dry dirt of Texas—it's rich in nutrients and made for plants like hydrangeas. If the hydrangea bush had blossomed in Texas, I was sure the possibilities here would be endless.

The first spring, I watched and waited. The bush grew tall and strong in the fertile soil. The leaves spread out and reached for the sunlight. But the blossoms? The beautiful, incredible flowers that had grown in abundance in Texas? They were nowhere in sight. There wasn't a single flower on any of the stems.

Next year will be better, I told myself. *I'm sure they'll bloom next spring.*

But they didn't. Not that year or the year after that or even the year after that. I tried everything. I amended the soil and bought fancy fertilizers and watered faithfully and cut back overhead branches to let in more sunlight. Nothing worked. The hydrangea bush refused to bloom.

One early spring morning five years into our journey, when dew still covered the grass, I walked out into the garden with a cup of coffee. As I stepped onto the stone-covered path, I couldn't believe my eyes. There it was—pink and green and perched between a cluster of leaves, peeking its tiny head out with a wink.

My first Kentucky hydrangea bloom.

It was a reminder of the promise we'd been given when we heard

God's call and jumped in search of a new life and a new adventure and new horizons. And it was a promise for the road ahead. It was a promise for all the days that had gone before and all the days that were yet to come.

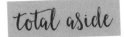

Noah had his rainbow. Jacob had his ladder. Sarah had her son. God knew I was a home and garden blogger, so he sent me a sign of his faithfulness in the form of flowers instead.

Those blooms were a tangible reminder that God's promises to us are new every day. He loves us with a love that is beyond all comprehension. He will never leave us or abandon us. He walks beside us every step of the way.

In that flower garden, with the sunlight dancing across the wet grass and the clouds drifting lazily in the blue sky and the flowers blooming with the promise of new life, I finally knew we were home.

It has been ten years since we sat in that church pew in Texas. Ten years since a red lipstick–loving, yoga pants–wearing, messy bun–haired woman and her husband decided to gather up their nearest and dearest, pack up the minivan, and drive hundreds of miles across the country into the unknown.

When we began our adventure years ago, I knew God had a purpose for all this. I knew beyond a shadow of a doubt there was a plan.

I didn't know the what or the why or the where or even the how of the design. Truthfully, it all made me a little scared and a little nervous. It was intimidating to step out in faith without a script, without knowing where the journey would lead.

We simply had to trust.

To obey.

To jump.

Looking back now, I see the purpose more clearly. I see more of the plan. In each of the steps of the jump, God has taught my heart, giving me the wisdom to open my eyes to my weaknesses and the courage to embrace my strengths. Along the way, he has been shaping me and refining me and allowing me to grow in ways I never could have imagined.

I have learned to find joy in my imperfections and to embrace the dings and scratches of life. Even though I am cracked and imperfect and nicked and worn and weary, the Potter has a plan. He is molding me into something perfectly imperfect. He delights in taking a broken vessel and using me for his design.

I have discovered that it takes courage to open to a knock at the door. Opening a door can be scary. I know. Dream following can be overwhelming. When faced with what we have hoped and dreamed and prayed for, we are often reluctant to embrace what is right in front of us. But we serve a God whose plans are so much more amazing than our own.

I have learned along the journey to die a little more to self. To humble myself (and my pot roast) and recognize how much I have to learn from my new neighbors. They have opened my eyes to the value of friendship and encouragement and the generosity of hospitality.

I have learned that worry and doubt are overrated and that it's foolish to waste a moment on things that are out of my control. God, in his infinite mercy, has determined the direction and the steps on this journey. He knows. He understands. He is the one who led us to the country, and he is still making our path straight. All that is required of us is to place our faith in him.

⌒ɲɔ

I learned one of life's simplest, but most important, lessons in the most ordinary of places. It was wrapped up in a potato skin and left to harden under the floor mat in the backseat of our car. Never underestimate the parable that can be found in a petrified piece of complex carbohydrate.

Our minivan was full of them: pieces of stale potato chips, half-eaten chicken nuggets, deflated Cheetos, and icing-covered lions missing the occasional front paw. I was never really sure how all that junk food ended up wedged between the seats, tucked under the floor mats, and crushed into the cup holders. Whenever I asked who left the smashed banana on the floor or who had stuffed the half-eaten granola bar into the pocket behind the seat, the answer was always the same.

Nobody.

That unsavory character and his friends No One, Not Me, and I Don't Know left behind a path of crumbs and destruction all across the backseat of our vehicle. It was uncanny. The more I'd clean up the mess, the more the mess would grow. I was winning the battle and losing the snack-food war.

One Sunday, after we had been in Kentucky for several years, we

The amazing doesn't usually jump out at you in the big, flashy moments. It often tiptoes in through the back door.

pulled into the worship center parking lot after a hectic pre-church morning. I glanced into the backseat and scanned the small humans one last time before we opened the car door. My heart sank. My daughter's bow was hanging on by a thread, my older son had on a wrinkled shirt with a missing button, and his younger brother was using his shoes as puppets to entertain his siblings.

I fixed and fluffed and buttoned and tied shoes until I felt we were ready to face the public. At last, I opened the side door of the van. All four children piled out in a rush, running through the church doors and leaving behind a spray of cookie crumbs, crackers, and petrified french fries. Those fries, hardened into a substance stronger than Superman's arms of steel, escaped the confines of the car and bounced along the pavement in rapid succession.

They were taunting me.

I could practically hear them giggling, laughing in glee as they made their maniacal journey across the sidewalk.

Embarrassed, I looked around to see if anyone was watching. Then I scooped up the fries and dumped them into the trash can before anyone noticed. I felt inadequate and unorganized and discouraged over my inability to control a single one of the food groups.

After I brushed off the crumbs and picked up a few stray juice box containers, I closed the door to the van. Pausing to gather my thoughts, I straightened my skirt, checked my red lipstick in the passenger side mirror, twirled an unruly curl back into place, and turned to go inside. Then, out of the corner of my eye, something caught my attention.

As I glanced into the front seat of the car next to me, I couldn't believe it. It was perfect—not a crumb or a piece of paper or a petrified piece of anything anywhere. Every sparkle was sparkling. Every piece of lint had been banished from the car's presence. Every floor mat was clean, with the tiny vacuum lines still in place. The freshly oiled leather glinted in the morning sun, and there, in the pocket behind the seat, where I'd just noticed the remnants of a forty-eight-pack of crayons in my own car, was a perfectly perfect umbrella.

Simply waiting for a rainy day.

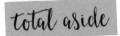

I once tried keeping an umbrella in my car for emergencies. I bought a tiny contraption that folded down to nothing, and I kept it in the glove compartment. It was the best of plans . . . until I tried to use it. The first time I opened it, the spokes parted ways, and the sides of the umbrella totally ruined my perfect-hair day. So much for being ready for a rainy day.

I think it was the umbrella that sent me over the edge. I longed with my heart and several other organs for the perfection of that car with its all-weather gear. I wanted a car with shiny seats and clean floor mats and sparkling windows without fingerprints. A car where petrified french fries would never, ever dare to show their faces.

With one last wistful look at perfection, I headed into the building. Sighing to myself, I headed to my Sunday school room with visions of sparkly cars still dancing in my head.

And then I saw her. The owner of the umbrella-pocket car.

There she sat, patiently waiting for her class to start. She was an older woman, poised and beautiful and dressed to perfection. Not a hair was out of place.

I glanced down at my wrinkled dress with crumbs still clinging to the hem and tentatively reached up to straighten my sweater. She was everything I hoped to be, everything I aspired to. I couldn't help it. I had to say something.

"I love your car," I blurted out. "I was sitting in my car full of crayons and crushed juice boxes and dried-up pieces of fast food." My words tumbled out in a rush. "And then I saw your car, and I almost cried. It's perfect and wonderful and clean and sparkling *and . . . and . . . and . . .* you have an umbrella," I finished.

She didn't say a word. She just smiled a little sadly.

In the silence that ensued after my outburst, I stood there, smiling awkwardly and not knowing what to say next. Finally, I waved and started making my way to class.

On my way down the hall, one of her friends pulled me aside and whispered to me in a small voice that pierced to the center of my heart. "She would trade with you in a minute."

The truth of that simple whisper almost sent me to my knees.

She was right.

So wisely, perfectly, wonderfully, incredible-reminder-at-the-exact-moment-you-need-it, take-your-breath-away right. Time passes so quickly, and the days of crayons and crumbs and french fries soon fade away.

One moment they are there. Then you blink.

And they're gone.

As I walked away, I counted every blessing and then sent up a silent prayer of gratitude. Gratitude for little hands that reached for mine and joyful voices that chattered and giggled and told knock-knock jokes while carrying around handfuls of chicken nuggets and cookie crumbs.

And I was grateful for what I'd learned that day. This is the life lesson I want to print on my heart: there is such joy in the journey.

$\sim\!\!\gamma\!\!\circ$

When we left our home and everything that was familiar to chase a dream, we were seeking amazing. We were looking for an amazing adventure, an amazing new home in the country, an amazing well-adjusted family, an amazing new way to grow our own wheat. But we discovered that the amazing wasn't really found in the big moments. In the flash. In the sparkle. In the fireworks.

Instead, it often tiptoed in through the back door.

The amazing came in the form of nails that were pried from an antique floor, in the broken window that had been tossed aside on the curb, in a pot roast that didn't know its place, in ever-rising floodwaters, in the roar of a dinosaur, and in the tiny petals of a hydrangea bloom.

Every step. Every minute. Every mile. Every lesson. Every heartbeat.

We had no way of knowing, but we had been so close to amazing . . . all along.

In-Spite-of-All-Odds Mason Jar Vase

SUPPLIES

+ 1 mason jar
+ 1 wire mason jar hanger
+ 1 piece of wood
  (1 inch by 4 inches by 8 inches)
+ 1 hook *(3 inches long)*

+ screwdriver
+ 1 screw *(½ inch long)*
+ fresh flowers
  (preferably hydrangeas)

196

1. Wash the mason jar, and let it dry.

2. Wrap the wire hanger around the rim of the mason jar.

3. Place the piece of wood in a vertical position, center the hook in the middle of the wood, and screw it in.

4. Hang the wood with the attached hook to an outdoor fence post, a fence board, or even next to the front door.

5. Place the mason jar on the hook, and fill it with flowers.

6. Remind yourself that you are amazing, and take a moment to smell the flowers.

epilogue

I'm sitting here on the back porch of the farmhouse smelling spring. I can't help it. It's everywhere. The hay is ready to be cut in the back pasture, and fluffy blue clouds are floating by overhead, and the birds are chirping in the dogwood trees, and the cows are making sounds that remind me of the *Love Boat*'s horn. Or maybe the honk of the plane on *Fantasy Island*. Or maybe both.

Just an ordinary setting of the sun in Kentucky.

And yet in the middle of all this spring and hay and clouds and chirping birds and noise-making cows, I can't shake the feeling that change is in the air too. I don't know when, and I don't know where, and I don't know how, but I don't think the winding road ends here. I don't think this is our last jump. I don't think this is the last chapter in our story.

The rest of the journey is as yet unwritten.

See, that's the thing about God. He is mighty. He is sovereign.

His ways are not our own. The plans he makes for us and the paths he directs us down are often closer to amazing than we can even imagine. And I know that I know that I know that God isn't finished with our family yet.

But today I'll wriggle my desperately-needing-a-pedicure toes in the blades of new grass and listen to turkeys gobbling from across the meadow and sip sweet tea with lime. Today I'll call my mother-in-law and ask what her secret snickerdoodle ingredient is. Today I'll listen to my husband play the guitar and smile at my children's laughter.

I'll let today be today . . . and simply wait for tomorrow.

about the author

KariAnne writes the decorating and lifestyle blog *Thistlewood Farms* from the back porch of her vintage farmhouse in the rolling hills of Kentucky. She followed God's call and jumped with her family from the busy Dallas metroplex to the middle of the country, where she lives with her husband and four children.

If you turn down the winding country road to KariAnne's farmhouse, you might find her painting mismatched chairs, listening to the music of the crickets in the pasture, singing Scripture, or walking hand in hand with her knight-in-shining-armor husband as the sun sets over the river. She loves sweet tea with lime, thunderstorms, good books, milk glass, and yard sales, and she is an imperfect DIY-er saved by grace.

Thistlewood Farms is full of stories of family and faith and features hundreds of the home decor projects that KariAnne creates every week for readers. The blog was awarded the *Country Living* Decorating Blog of the Year and was named one of the Top 10 Decorating

Blogs by *Better Homes and Gardens*. She has been featured in *Better Homes and Gardens Christmas Ideas*, *Country Living*, *Flea Market Décor*, *Country Woman*, *HGTV Magazine*, the *Cottage Journal*, the *Chicago Tribune*, *Reloved*, and *This Old House* magazine, and on popular websites including *The Today Show*, *Better Homes and Gardens*, *Country Living*, *Apartment Therapy*, *Good Housekeeping*, *Mediakix*, *Bob Vila*, and *BuzzFeed*. KariAnne has made appearances on television programs including Nashville's NewsChannel 5's *Talk of the Town* and Channel 8 in Dallas, and her blog was voted one of the best DIY blogs of 2015.

THE DIY
(DECORATE IT YOURSELF)
HOME PLANNER

You've read KariAnne's story, and now she wants to help you *design* yours. Her home planner will be your **go-to guide** to make your decorating dreams come true with...

Inspiration to
get you started

Tips for windows, walls,
furniture, floors... *and more!*

Answers to your
decorating questions

Pockets to hold paint chips,
fabric samples, etc.

Adorable artwork, graph paper,
and helpful diagrams

This book is a reference guide, organizer, and notebook—all in one!

Online Discussion *guide*

TAKE *your* TYNDALE READING EXPERIENCE *to the* NEXT LEVEL

A FREE discussion guide for this book is available at bookclubhub.net, perfect for sparking conversations in your book group or for digging deeper into the text on your own.

www.bookclubhub.net

You'll also find free discussion guides for other Tyndale books, e-newsletters, e-mail devotionals, virtual book tours, and more!